The Golden Precepts

from

The Book of Life

Embodying the wisdom of the eternal ages

transcribed
by
AURA MAY HOLLEN

Published by
HENRY HOLLEN, M.D.
Los Angeles, California

PRINTED IN U.S.A.
PIONEER PRINTING CO.
GLENDALE, CALIF.

WITHIN THE ORACLE
LIETH WISDOM
AND WITHIN WISDOM
LIETH ILLUMINATION

PART ONE

The Golden Precepts

Oracle One

Unto him who yearneth cometh the spirit of the Living Christ. Thus is established communion. Soul, casting off the fetters of materialistic instinct, centereth its longing on the attainment of the Divine.

He who seeketh in material pleasure to quench his thirst, slaketh not. Parched, he traverseth the desert of defeated hope, glimpsing but the oasis of his own desire. He who turneth to the fount which ever floweth, drinking from the Living Waters, knoweth the joy of fulfilment.

Turn ye from the path of diversified pleasure. For herein are found but the ashes of despair.

Man in his temerity knocketh at the door of opportunity. It openeth not, barring entrance. Doth he cast aside his yearning? He maketh repeated attempt, forcing the will to respond. Thus is material instinct delineated.

The soul which turneth to the Divine, inspired by Spirit's urge, is as the flower which lifteth to the sun its petals, receiving that which bringeth to perfection its effort.

Glamorous the lure which desire imposeth. It is as a tinsel robe which veileth the dross beneath. The flowing drapery, brushing the surface of indulgence, raiseth the dust which blinds the eye to purity. Long and devious the course the selfish soul pursueth ere cometh comprehension of the futility of error.

Error is the distorted image of selfish purpose, satiation being the aftermath of indulgence.

The flower of purity bloometh not by the wayside, accessible to the casual passerby. It groweth in the Garden of Divinity, which soul reacheth through the path of renunciation, this being the Cross upon which the self crucifieth desire.

Thou who art seeking, giving heed to the silent voice of Spirit, permit not the darkness which enfolds thee to lessen thy faith. Ever doth the darkness precede the dawn, which is as the illumination of soul when through faith it penetrateth the fog of superstition and fear, which are as a barrier to growth.

If a shadow cross thy path, barring from thee the sun of love, think not it is of grave consequence. Within it lieth a lesson, a page which thou must scan with far vision until in it is revealed the purpose. Perchance a weakness hath become manifest, which thy soul must eradicate through the process of self-analysis. The testing of the metal denoteth the presence of the dross. The golden ore must needs through refining become the purified substance.

Soul, subject to the law of birth and rebirth, trendeth its way through innumerable schools of experience ere it casteth aside the fetters of materialistic longing, which are as a barrier to growth. The River of Time runneth fast on the plane of physical interpretation. It mergeth in the Ocean of Eternity when evolution is complete.

The sands of the sea countless are to the mind hampered by the physical organism. Weighed on the scales of divine comprehension, each infinitesimal grain standeth apart, a perfect whole in the final analysis.

The mosaic of Eternity denoteth the divine pattern. Each soul in physical being is as a part which must needs be completed, that in spiritual counterpart it fit the exact requirement demanded.

Each twig on the mighty oak becomes, in the course Time denoteth, the hardened branch. Thus soul evolves from incipient being into the selfless status.

The law of evolution turneth the cycle of Time, with unerring precision apportioning the exact experience soul needeth that growth be consistent with progress.

Destiny, man calleth the scythe with which Time reapeth; Death, the sinister title by which the adolescent designateth this, the messenger of love.

Love maketh entrance in a diversity of guise, propelled by the divine understanding which motivateth being. Hatred maketh entrance disguised as love, until understanding teareth apart the tinsel robe which masks; revealing in nakedness lust, which is ever a near kin to deceit. Know thy companions, lest through adverse influence thy soul make obeisance at the false shrine of evil intent.

As a shadow cast over thee is that which adverse thought reflecteth unless thou wear the armour of peace, which deflects the shafts of antagonistic regard.

Know well thyself. For each debt which soul contracteth must be obviated through thine own effort.

Thou art as a mirror which reflecteth the image of desire. Blurred and opaque may be the impression. Or clear-cut as a jewel, scintillating with brilliancy, may be the replica of thy yearning.

Guard well thy speech. For within it lie the seeds of thought which thou art sowing. In proportion wilt thou reap a harvest of joy or the empty tares of sorrow and despair.

Man reapeth not alone. Countless souls through proximity partake of the seeds cast into the fertile soil of human endeavor. Like to like, denoteth the law of equality. Be it of evil or purity, of constructive or destructive tendency, the law operateth relentlessly, thrusting upon soul the necessity for rebuilding with the tools of comprehensive self-analysis.

Man thrusteth the sword of retaliatory measure within the companionate soul. It reboundeth, the incision tearing apart the tissue of resistance which encaseth the morale.

The consciousness retaineth all that mind imprinteth therein, until through the sieve of comprehension soul sifts the ashes of adverse thought from the living embers of pure intent.

As a flower bendeth to the wind which blows, so soul maketh obeisance to the god of its innate yearning.

Experience teacheth a diversity of lessons. It maketh of soul a Temple whose altar is accessible to diversified emotion, each through the portal of desire making entrance to light the taper of temporary indulgence.

Permit not the oasis of a restricted creed to lure thee when traversing the desert of blasted hope. Thy soul will not thus reach its journey's end. Pause a brief moment, absorbing that which quencheth thy thirst, realizing that the desert is but the intervening span which separates thee from thy eternal home.

Man drinketh from the goblet of despair. But the turbulent depths reveal, when the draught is complete, the pure crystal beneath.

Oracle Two

A rose bloometh upon the parent bush, its petals reflecting the glory of the eternal dawn. Man seeth in it a rare loveliness. But, unless Spirit illumine soul, he glimpseth not the image of the Divine.

Soul through yearning must approach the source of the Divine ere to it is given the power of perception. Thus the enlightened soul glimpseth the immortal handiwork.

The wind whispereth through space, bearing within its balmy breath a promise of peace. Man seeth not its content unless in destructive effort it leaveth devastation in its path.

The desert symbolic is of the barren soul which, lacking the fertility of understanding, receiveth not the seeds of divinity.

The flower which bloometh for a day leaveth its aroma imprinted within the consciousness. Man saith its brief life hath accomplished naught. Within the Eternal Records is imprinted the replica of its conception.

Hither and yon bloweth the straw, with naught to stabilize its course. Thus the soul lacking spiritual impetus respondeth to the urge of desire, in varying currents of emotion bruising its content.

The blue ether denoteth immeasurable distance. Space lieth only within the confines mind designates; the Immortal, with the perceptive vision, penetrating all with the ease of concentrative effort.

Man speaketh in childish vein, refuting that which

the physical vision encompasseth not. When understanding quickens the tempo of the spiritual pulse the idle chatter is revealed as the magpie's effort. The advanced soul through reticence denoteth its strength. Impregnable the reserve with which soul erects the protective barrier.

The eternal dawn promiseth the fulfilment of the soul's yearning. But he who seeketh therein the Mecca of fulfilment must through renunciation cast aside selfish purpose.

The lark wingeth its path joyously, breathing the divine melody. Within each note is glimpsed the harmonic tone of the spheres, which echoes ceaselessly throughout the universal kingdom.

Man denieth that which he heareth not. But the mind, which invisible is, lending itself not to dissection, recordeth with unfailing precision each errant thought within the consciousness, there embedded until through concentrative analysis its value is weighed on the scales of divine comprehension.

Error hideth beneath the veil of illusion, whose tinsel draperies tarnish when the consciousness demandeth a cleansing of its turbid content.

Illusion is the false friend whose promise is brittle as the thread which breaks when the strain of reality measureth its innate strength.

The spectre of Death terrifieth the soul whose foundation rests upon that which superstition hath builded.

Life thrusts the goblet of fulfilment within the hand of the initiate. Gazing within its translucent depths, the tincture of joy mergeth into the peace of a supreme content.

The tinkling brass denoteth the speech of the adolescent whose yearning concentrateth on the attainment of the material. The acid test revealeth the faulty metal, the pure gold buried beneath the alloy of a false creed.

Creed is that which restricteth thought, building the barrier of an adverse and intolerant judgment. As the snow melteth beneath the ardent rays of the sun, so shall be merged in the Universal these, the chains which fetter the mind.

A star gleameth within the superlative heights, luring with its promise of divinity. Until the mind accepts the laws of a spiritual universe its hunger remaineth unappeased, with the loaf of fulfilment as remote as the celestial wanderer.

Humility is the robe with which the advanced soul enwrappeth the self. He who stalketh in his pride trails the false garment of an egotistic learning.

The cleansing process denoteth the manner through which the consciousness is fertilized, that within its soil be implanted the seeds of reconstructive effort.

Man speaketh glibly of the law of eternal consequence. The Master-Physician with unerring precision weigheth each word on the scales of understanding, giving ample measure if soul yearneth but through weakness balances not the content of its effort.

As a monstrous sore is the greed which covereth the surface of the mass-mind. The curative measure denoteth a castigation with the tincture of sorrow and despair.

Within the Garden of Divinity bloometh the rose of purity. Each petal denoteth the supreme workmanship of an immortal soul, motivated through the divine impulse, which is in reality the cosmic essence of love.

The chain which bindeth to error the soul of evil proclivity is that which selfish desire hath builded. Only through satiation, accompanied by a profound disillusionment, will the links through a metamorphosis be transformed into the etheric essence of a divine aura.

The aura delineates the spiritual essence which soul exudes as a rare fragrance of indescribable loveliness, this being as the robe of divine significance which denoteth the attainment of the spiritual analysis.

Compassion is the flower of love which findeth its inception in understanding.

He who knoweth love condemneth not, for within the understanding manifest he seeth all who err as babes in the school evolution provides for growth.

Condemnation findeth its source in hatred, whose near of kin is jealousy.

Man knoweth not love if he taketh from his brother. For love taketh not, but giveth of its all.

What matter if the soul on life's highway be as a bud which bloometh in the desolation of the desert. Its brief existence spent, the fragrance lingers on to enhance the lives of those as yet unborn. Thus descendeth, when necessity demands, the soul whose life reflects the divine radiance, to illumine the path for those who grope in the darkness of a spiritual disbelief.

Within the chaos of a universal unrest the Light permeateth, that humanity may take cognizance of the infinite compassion which emanates from the source of the Divine. The Light which cast its radiance over

Bethlehem illumineth the path which countless souls must trend as the ultimate achievement.

The wind sigheth as it bloweth through space. As a lullaby it breathes of peace. But harsh its note when the tempest denotes the presence of a Supreme Power. Thus the Omnipotent God demonstrateth His strength, that man undergo the ultimate of experience.

Strength is that through which power is expressed. Tempered, it worketh for good. Unrepressed, it is an adverse agent.

The Law denoteth order. He who liveth within the Law knoweth not fear. For harmony is the key-note to which the soul responds. The Law bodeth ill for the transgressor. For the path of indulgence leadeth in the veiled distance to the blank wall of a profound despair.

The golden grain denoteth the perfected harvest. The empty tares reveal the blighted seeds.

Civilization embraceth a multitude of souls, *humanity* being the name applied by the mass-mind. He who knoweth not the instinct of self-preservation is as a leaf which is carried on the breeze of desire to the remote distance of the arid waste. Only through the divine instinct will humanity be transposed from the mediocre to the sublime.

The elementary embraceth the incipient knowledge. The profound delineateth the supreme accomplishment. Herein lieth the path which soul traverses from the infancy of adolescence to the maturity of intellectuality.

He who garners his grain when the harvest denoteth fulfilment knoweth the joy of achievement. He who tarries until the chill wind of winter demandeth repose hath but the husks with which to satisfy his hunger.

Thus readeth the law of consequence, being in reality the Golden Oracle.

Oracle Three

Compassion denoteth the essence of understanding. It findeth its source in love, its healing power being manifest in an increased strength.

He who giveth in love receiveth in proportion to that which he bestows. He who withholdeth is stripped barren as the stalk devoid of the verdant green.

Pride is as a barrier to growth. It inflicteth upon the soul a burden whose weight depletes the strength until the fount denoteth naught of content.

The green pasture offereth a haven to him who walketh in love. The barren desert affordeth naught to satisfy the hunger of him who stalketh with hatred as an inseparable companion.

Soul extendeth its tendrils within the soil of love. But stunted its growth when the barren ground of racial discord barreth the sun of hope.

The well of wisdom floweth; immeasurable its content. But he who drinketh from its Living Waters must first cleanse soul of the prejudice of disbelief.

Faith is the key which openeth the portals of divine comprehension. The mind which barreth entrance is as a room with naught to admit the rays of the gleaming sun.

Man seeketh to penetrate the mystery of creative being. Unless his yearning be purged of selfish instinct the blank wall of a prejudicial belief bars his efforts to make entrance.

History recordeth that which man hath achieved. Within its content lie the combined efforts of countless souls. He who readeth with the spiritual vision glimpses between each line the working of the karmic principle, which denotes the cause which underlieth the effect.

Humility provideth a garment of rare loveliness. It enwrappeth the soul as a petal adorneth the golden heart of the rose.

Man saith: within the rose lieth the result of a profound culture. The Immortal saith: here is delineated the divine instinct which created the symbol of eternal beauty.

Seeking diligently, soul findeth the enigma of being. Scanning with the spiritual vision, the mystery lieth revealed. The cosmic universe it is which provideth life for all existent atoms.

Infinitesimal the grain of sand; microscopic its content. But upon its crystallized surface is imprinted the image of the Divine.

Divinity compriseth the elements of religious belief. It discardeth creed and sect as a barrier to progress, merging in the Universal all existent philosophies whose radiance enhances thought.

To the Supreme Intelligence must we turn for the wherewithal of being. Here lieth the source of the soul's nucleus, the divine element whose Light illumineth the soul, giving impetus for expression.

Thought is the invisible means through which soul expresseth. To analyze this, the intangible force which motivates being, is akin to making of the wind a captive, leashing it to the plough with which to till the soil.

Science demandeth proof of all that exists, placing beneath the microscope its varying content. Mind, elusive, maketh not obeisance to the dictum of the decree imposed.

Blind the soul which turneth from the spiritual interpretation of being, focussing its vision on that alone which presenteth tangible evidence.

As a parched and dreary world would be that which delineated not the verdant texture. Thus is the soul whose Light is dimmed by the dense fog of a restricting creed.

Creed imposeth a wall which barreth entrance to the realm of diversified thought. It is as a brook which floweth through a straight and narrow channel outlined by the concrete wall of a restricting barrier.

The brook which babbles noisily giveth forth little to enhance the landscape. The stream which floweth silently to the sea murmurs not, but through its intensity commandeth a profound respect.

He who seeketh in the mirror of reality to glimpse soul's reflection seeth that which inspires to increased effort for understanding. He who looketh in the mirror of an egotistic self-satisfaction seeth reflected the replica of his own desire.

Reality is that which exists, the unadorned foundation which supporteth thought. Unreality is that which the mind visions as a mirage with which to palliate desire.

The ashes of a depleted fire give scant measure of warmth. Thus is the soul which in selfishness refuseth to heed the call of his needy brother.

Charity is the giving in love to the needy soul, withholding naught which healeth with the essence of compassion.

Famine denoteth the absence of that with which to satisfy the hunger. Plenty demonstrateth the fullness of the need satisfied. Luxury indicateth the waste of plenty and surplus combined.

As a bee gathereth the nectar of the flower that the somnolescence of winter findeth the store of plenty, so the enlightened soul storeth within the consciousness that which sustains when the chill mantle of Death enwrappeth the physical through which soul manifests.

Life indicateth the fullness of being. Death delineateth the transposition to the etheric analysis. Birth giveth soul the opportunity for additional experience. Rebirth affords the diversified process through which soul interchangeth its garment, that from spiritual to physical interpretation it vary in endless continuity.

The wise man speaketh in parable, masking his wisdom as the shell which enwrappeth the kernel of the nut. The fool through exposure of the kernel enwrappeth not with the shell of intellectual ability, revealing his ignorance to derision.

Venomous the tongue of the slanderer, piercing the armour of the recipient with the rapier of a false insinuation. Defenseless the target, for humanity turneth ever from truth, seeking in a lie to disrobe purity of its radiance.

Purity indicateth the absence of the impure, the gold which through refinement hath had extracted the dross. Impurity delineateth the mixture of the obscene with the elements of a debauched taste, which seeketh in expression to disburse its content within the mass-mind.

As a drop of ink discoloreth the crystal-clearness of the filled goblet, so the unclean mind reflecteth the image of a perverted soul.

Like to like—readeth the law of propinquity. Thus the beast seeketh the beast; the flower the corresponding element. The soul clingeth to its companionate affinity. But within the scale of evolution the advance must of necessity indicate the ascent to a higher status. Thus the mass-consciousness provides the means through which the advance taketh place. In reality, it becometh the ladder by which each kingdom riseth to the ultimate.

The field flower looketh at the rose, which likewise turneth to the sun. Thus is reflected the divine urge which motivateth being.

The source of power lieth in the faith manifest. He who turneth to the Light instinctively reflects its radiance. He who turneth to the darkness liveth in the gloom of a restricted mind.

The Light which findeth its source in the Divine alone giveth to soul the power of vision. He who denieth the Light looketh through the darkened lens of an opaque thickness.

Oracle Four

The Light which illumines soul cometh from within. Thus is Spirit exemplified. Spirit, which partaketh of the Divine, denotes an integral part of the Great Whole which sustaineth the universe in harmonic accord.

Universality is that which embodies all that existeth. All creeds through unity shall become universal, discarding that which conflicts with truth, retaining that which is founded on fact.

Creed is the invisible barrier which separateth the soul from the field of diversified thought, erecting a wall of prejudice which soul is powerless to surmount.

Philosophy is the designation which man giveth to a profound and intricate theory. Dissected with the powerful lens of a concentrative analysis, its foundation sustaineth the mind which seeks in analytical effort to absorb its content.

The universe composeth the structure of integral being. It denotes a combined unity of all existent matter. Soul, functioning as an independent organ, partaketh of a fractional part. Infinitesimal its content when measured from the standard of a diversified whole.

The problem which confuseth the scientific mind, which accepts naught but that which delineates tangible evidence, lendeth itself with crystal-clearness to the spiritual vision, which with the microscope of divine interpretation penetrates the utmost depths.

It availeth naught in the final analysis whether soul function beneath that which racial prejudice designates as the Ethiopian or whether the Caucasian giveth substance to experience. Soul is weighed on the scales of universal import, which taketh cognizance of neither color nor creed.

The elemental of knowledge compriseth the ability to concentrate upon a given text, absorbing the composition of its content. The basic foundation of wisdom delineateth the ability to extract from the heterogeneous accumulation of knowledge the active principle, applying it to the theory exemplified.

Man knoweth not the hour when the summons cometh. He worketh in the vineyard of experience, draining from the goblet of life its foaming content. Whether he drain the dregs, or within the depths find the sparkling effervescence of peace, dependeth upon the mixture of which he hath blended the brew.

The desert of hope portrayeth a garden of indescribable loveliness. The immortal rose adorneth its wide expanse. He who fortifies the soul by wearing this, the symbol of purity, hath entered through the portals of enlightenment the Garden of the Gods.

The rose symbolic is of achievement. It exemplifies the ultimate of attainment. The advanced soul appraiseth its rare loveliness with the vision growth bestows. The adolescent weareth it as an adornment with which to intrigue the senses.

The perfume of Paradise exudeth from the rose, this being in reality the spiritual essence of a divine masterpiece.

The Oriental philosophy denoteth a collection of rare jewels, each enwrapped within the gossamer veil of illusion. The soul which yearneth must first unwrap each flawless gem from its enveloping fold ere the brilliancy of the jewel enhances his consciousness.

Illusion provideth the veil with which the near-initiate protects his soul. It formeth a buffer between soul and the harsh wind of reality, which strips truth of that which enhances but depreciates its content.

An angel in disguise is Sorrow who masqueradeth as adversity. The flowing robes of sombre hue are transformed into the radiant aura of a sublime significance when soul through renunciation recognizeth the celestial visitor.

The Christic principle embraceth the fundamentals of love, tolerance, compassion and understanding. Combined, they delineate selflessness, this being the ultimate of all existent souls.

The wind of adversity bloweth with cyclonic intensity when necessity demands. Thus the Divine Will operateth, that humanity take cognizance of its predominating weakness.

Man sigheth with remorse when through sorrow he tasteth the bitter aloe of defeated purpose. But the draught, which must be drained to fulfilment, is the brew he hath blended with the nectar he hath taken from his brother.

Thievery denotes the process of attaching to the self that which belongeth to another. The law readeth: covet not that which is not thine own lest retribution lead thee to the scaffold which thine own act hath builded.

The Golden Rule exemplifieth the law of universal brotherhood. He who liveth within its ancient boundary hath with far vision embraced the active principle of divine comprehension.

The source of the Divine lieth within the Spirit's urge. It impelleth soul to expression, thus thrusting apart the portals of yearning through which soul enters the sacred precincts of communion.

Communion is the means through which soul freeth the self from the fetters the physical universe imposes, ascending to the realm of spiritual interpretation, there through unity to become merged in the Universal.

Cosmic the universe and all that existeth therein, this being the means through which the Divine Will is expressed.

The sands of the sea change ceaselessly, being motivated by the tide of eternal consequence. Thus soul giveth response to the Law, which demands that experience provide the wherewithal for growth.

The ocean exemplifieth the Great Whole within which all subsidiary streams find submergence. Thus the Universal Mind absorbs the individual soul when through evolution it returneth to the source of its being.

The tide turneth when through magnetic control it hath exemplified the Law. Thus soul reverseth its course when through experience it hath come into a comprehension of the futility of error.

The scythe of Time moweth relentlessly the flotsam of humanity, its blade delineating the rapier's strength. But the barren soil which remains shall be impregnated with a new growth that another harvest ripen into renewed being, thus exemplifying the law of rebirth.

The adolescent soul refutes the law of rebirth, finding within its tenets that which inspireth fear. He seeth dissolution as a monstrous error which Nature produces.

מצרים [מ] .י

The advanced soul seeth the discarding of the physical garment as the dawn of a new spring through which Nature bringeth to fruition the decadent somnolescence of autumnal proclivity.

The pearl standeth for purity because of its opalescent tendency. It through evolution clarifieth its robe, giving forth the sparkling clearness of the flawless gem.

The mineral kingdom produceth the analysis for evolution. It maketh the ascent from the lifeless clod of clay to the sparkling brilliancy of the diamond. Thus the mass-consciousness harbors evolution.

The drop of crystal-clearness which clingeth to the pane, a moment hence droppeth to oblivion. Thus the soul whom fame hath crowned with the false diadem of achievement, which bursteth as a bubble, absorbed through dissolution within the oblivion of memory's discard.

Memory is that through which man recollects the past. Ever and anon, Time with gentle hand brusheth the surface of the mind, erasing the imprint that a fresh page be given on which to record experience.

The consciousness receiveth the imprint of thought. It resembles a chest in which mind storeth its waste and its treasure. When filled to completement soul through adversity, accompanied by sorrow, sifteth the content, retaining but that which enhances. Thus the Law operateth.

Colossal the esteem with which the egotist regardeth the self. Pricked with the needle of adversity, it is as a bubble which bursts, with naught remaining but the prism which reflecteth the Divine.

The rainbow exemplifies the veil with which Nature enwrappeth creation. Thus is soul enhanced by the aura, which is in reality its outer garment.

The blind seeth not that of which it is a part. Thus motivates the soul which refutes the spiritual antithesis of being.

Reality provideth the means for Spirit's exemplification. Unreality giveth to soul the opportunity for experience. Man confuseth reality with unreality until through the portals of death he enters the plane of comprehensive analysis, when his vision embraceth that which he hath renounced.

The snail propels the self laboriously, progress being impeded by its enveloping shell. The soul through derision refutes the source of its being until, through the crushing of the shell, it perforce must motivate of its own volition.

The camel drinketh not on its long journey across the intervening sands. So doth the soul which clingeth to material desire refrain from accepting the divine brew that Spirit offers, with which to quench its thirst.

Thirst is the craving for that which giveth alleviation to desire. If the brew be filled with the salt of tears it relieveth not, but rather doth it exaggerate the yearning for satiation. Thus soul purgeth of its predominating weakness.

Strength denoteth the ability to withstand defeat. Weakness delineateth the absence of strength which motivates. To combine strength with initiative produceth endurance, which sustains effort.

The rose casteth aside its petals when its aroma is

exhausted. The heart of gold remaineth a mute testimony of its achievement. Thus the pure soul leaveth that whose fragrance enhances thought when in spiritual delineation it continueth its activity.

A million buds must burst ere is produced the perfected flower. But within each bud lieth a promise of fulfilment.

Generation succeedeth generation, the cultural instinct denoting an advance. If Time a laggard is and growth be not sustained, the lash of adversity teacheth Time the necessity for a profound analysis.

The cause lieth within the effect. The unthinking mind putteth the cart before the horse, thus striving to thread the camel through the needle's eye.

The needle denoteth a marked diversity of purpose. It pricketh that its power be manifest. It refuseth entrance if its blunt end be introduced. Thus the arrogant soul, which must needs be reversed that its utility be not impaired by a biased judgment.

Sarcasm produceth a weapon for retaliatory measure. It is as a blade with which the egotist woundeth his adversary, piercing the armour soul hath erected by tearing to shreds the self-esteem.

Oracle Five

The cameo denoteth the clear-cut facsimile of pure thought, which, imprinted within the consciousness, buildeth the foundation for the intellectual capacity. Adverse thought maketh that which, blurred and indistinct, is as the waste which mars the perfect mechanism of the mind.

The wheat ripeneth, each golden grain denoting the perfect whole. It formeth the integral part of the harvest. Thus soul, when a purified substance, becometh as one golden link in the divine chain of celestial being.

A chain through unity denoteth a multiple strength. If one link through frailty manifest a faulty workmanship, it endangers that of which it formeth a part. Thus one soul through adverse influence casteth a shadow over companionate souls. Herein lieth a debt which must be obviated.

The spider spinneth its web, enmeshing within its frail fabrication the unwary fly. Thus the greedy soul reacheth out, taking unto himself that which his brother prizeth.

Man exemplifieth the elements of hatred and love. Separated, one worketh a hardship to soul, thrusting upon it a burden of woe. Love lifteth hatred, embracing with compassion. But hatred destroyeth love, crushing with ignominy.

He who attempts to split a hair in controversial argument is as a ship which striveth to sail the sea with the ocean's content pouring through the aperture which delineates its fundamental weakness.

Man declaimeth the non-existence of the Supreme Intelligence. But when Sorrow knocketh at the portals

of his heart it is upon bended knees he beseecheth alleviation of his woe.

The blade of grass denoteth the intricate veining of
the Master's art. But the unseeing mind glimpseth but
the contour of its length, apportioning it through habit
to the field of inconsequential being.

The straw which spinneth haphazard within the prevailing current denoteth the inability for stabilization.
Similar is the adolescent whose mind whirleth as the
weather-vane in response to the urge of diversified desire.

The loaf indicateth the proverbial staff of life. But
unless embellished with an additional relish it proveth
a sorry diet. Thus is the soul which limits the thought-
stream to the channel the chosen creed defines.

Variety lendeth savour to life, be it in whatsoever
field represented. The dietary regimen demandeth a
diversity of food to promote a state of well-being. The
mental appetite requireth that which is as the caviar to
thought. The fanatic restricteth habit to that which his
peculiar taste outlines. Normalcy playeth not a part,
idiosyncrasy controlling action.

Blunt the ax when it hath devastated the mighty oak.
But sharp the blade when it cutteth apart the tender
shrub. Thus the mind reacts when the burden of a profound problem hath weighed its content to the depth
of weariness. As with the camel, it is the final straw
which breaketh the back.

The vertebrae support the intricate nerve-system
which motivateth action. To subtract from the human
organism this, its true support, is as to delete from
thought the religious content.

The Supreme Intelligence permeateth the universal concept of thought as the rays of the ardent sun illumine the darkened edifice. The eternal night giveth way to the eternal day when love gleameth through the darkness of the unenlightened mind.

Mind, facile and adaptable, lendeth itself to thought. To, through control, limit the quantity of the inconsequential, training it to receive that which uplifts, is akin to embellishing the dome of the Temple of Thought.

Man buildeth a temple which he dedicates to the Omnipotent God. He openeth the portals to all who will to enter. But he draweth the line of creed, demanding the supplicant to quench his thirst but with the brew offered by the predominating head. Plentiful the content but inadequate the brew.

Liberty composeth the ability of free choice. If a man give that which enriches but place upon it the padlock of individual control, it limits the recipient as the locked portal denieth entrance to the inflow of diversified thought.

The vagabond seeketh in charity that with which to alleviate his hunger. Cold as the glacier is the giver who bestoweth in hatred, with the priceless gift of compassion deleted from his bounty.

The hypocrite declaimeth his virtue, seeking to establish the precedent of love. But the far vision penetrates his disguise and seeth in its pitiful weakness a warped and suffering soul.

A lie reboundeth upon the perpetrator. It goeth in a circle. But ever it returneth on the cycle of its own momentum.

Sickness denoteth an error of thought. It is that which

soul hath builded through an innate weakness. The medical mind protests it cometh from disease. This is but another pseudonym for an infraction of the morale, the etheric counterpart exemplifying in exact replica the disorder of the physical.

Within the physical healing lieth the etheric substance. The Master-Physician healeth that through which soul expresses ere to the manifesting agent cometh alleviation of its woe.

Man looketh not to the Divine when life floweth in the harmony of desire achieved. It is when the backwash of sorrow breaketh the wall of resistance that he turneth to the Supreme God, seeking surcease of his pain.

Faith giveth the soul the strength to withstand the storm of life. But if faith be deficient, soul is as a leaf blown hither and yon, as powerless to alight as the feather in the breeze.

The feather lacketh that which denotes substance. Thus formeth the mind; through imperceptible degrees accumulating that which giveth weight to thought.

Thought, intangible, evanescent, eludeth the analytical process. It cometh, it goeth as the wind; inconsequential as a breeze or profound with multiple intensity. Soul alone, through its acquired or deficient strength, giveth to thought its inherent quality.

The weaver, with multiple thread, maketh the warp to support the fabric. Thus mind laboriously constructs that which upholdeth thought. According to the workmanship is the finished product.

The broken thread endangereth the completed fabric. The wise mechanic looketh to each knot before he calleth his task complete.

Man seeketh in reprisal to wound his adversary. What gaineth the soul through retaliatory measure?

The elephant masketh in bulk weight its deficient mentality. Thus the intellectual whose mind denieth the existence of a supreme and omnipotent God.

The divine healer is he who worketh in love. For love alone hath the power to permeate the afflicted soul.

Pain is as a surgeon's blade which cauterizeth the consciousness. It must of necessity enlarge the wound in order to establish the healing propensity.

He who looketh in thine eyes when he speaketh is as a spring whose hidden depths reveal the clear content of the soul. He who turneth from thee, unable through uprightness to meet thy gaze, strives to hide the inherent weakness which tormenteth in subconscious humiliation.

The peacock strutteth in pride, striving to parade its gorgeous plumage. Thus vanity crieth aloud for that with which to adorn its weakness.

To strip from the soul its inherent weakness is as to amputate from the physical organism a necessary member. The antidote of love acteth as a sedative, which giveth to soul the endurance the operation demands.

Life maketh entrance garbed in garments of sombre hue. Humanity crieth aloud, demanding the raiment of plenty. The Law readeth: famine and plenty walk not in close companionship.

Hunger driveth man to the commitment of crime. Plenty lureth to the achievement of folly. Which giveth to soul an increased fortitude? One depleteth strength. Whereas the other casteth a shadow of remorse. Canst thou differentiate?

Nature in diversified color lendeth to the floral kingdom a halo of beauty. Couldst thou vision a garden with naught of variety to enrapture the soul? It is through Nature thy Father calleth, giving to man a fleeting glimpse of the wonder of His art.

To the unthinking mind the waning sun denoteth a happenstance, its radiant colors blended to the artist's raptured gaze. To the soul whose understanding illumines mind the panorama is as a replica of Paradise, engraven on the ether with the unerring hand of love.

Love giveth to soul the power of expression. He who receiveth and shareth with humanity findeth his gift enriched a thousandfold. He who taketh his art, using it as a shrine from which he barreth public worship, is as a miser who in the gloomy vault counteth his gold, with naught but penury to animate desire.

He who giveth, withholding naught, findeth his coffers replenished when he deemeth the supply impoverished.

Soul demandeth a dispensation of its wealth. A surplus of love if not expended worketh a hardship on the mind.

Love compriseth the elements of divinity, being the tool with which the Supreme Mind buildeth the universe.

Oracle Six

The orthodox mind denoteth a tabernacle whose portals are sealed, permitting not the radiant rays of the gleaming sun to penetrate its gloom.

The tabernacle of divine construction openeth wide its portals to all who would enter in humility and love. It barreth neither color nor creed. For within the Fount of Absolution lieth that which cleanses soul, which goeth forth stripped of all but that which enhances thought.

Man in his ignorance draweth the line of caste, realizing not that the divine spark which illumines soul findeth its source in the Father, who createth all in the divine image which knoweth neither race nor creed.

Race giveth to soul the opportunity for diversified experience. It provideth the school in which humility is the predominating lesson taught. For without this, the flower of love, soul is as a goblet whose opaque thickness denoteth not the crystal of transparency.

Diversified the path which soul trendeth in its journey through the Cosmos. He who deviateth not, holding in thought the emblem of the Cross, facilitates growth. For at the foot doth he lay his burden down. And upon its widespread arms doth he crucify the self.

The Cross symbolic is of purity, for it denoteth the supreme sacrifice which the Christ exemplifies. He who clingeth to its barren structure findeth the enveloping arms as tender as a mother's breast.

Motherhood denotes that which giveth; nor withholdeth. It bringeth into being the newborn soul and it wrappeth the shroud when death intervenes, in the tears of divine tenderness.

The wind holdeth within its soft folds the mystery of being. It breathes balmy-sweet. Or it threatens in harsh tones of destruction. Whatsoever be the melody it gives, it findeth its source in love.

The top spinneth frantically when its momentum giveth speed. But it falleth to ignominy as the false impetus subsides. Thus the ascent to fame when adulation turneth the head with flattery's impetus.

Raillery supplieth the elements of mirth. But it soundeth as the shrill cackle of the feathered denizen when the thought interjected denotes the jealous instinct of the greedy soul.

Laughter giveth to soul the expression of joy. It lendeth support. For within it soul casteth off the burden of profound import. If practiced to excess it is as a supercharged battery which in collapse falleth to disgrace.

Man defineth as a falling from caste, virtue defiled. It is the physical indulgence of a perverse desire. The Supreme Intelligence saith: man sinneth in thought ere in physical gratification he lendeth strength to desire.

Desire it is through which soul expresseth. It may trend the sordid path of indulgence. Or it may elevate soul to the plane of divine conception.

As a man thinketh, so he is. He speaketh words of wisdom. Or he giveth to humanity the false gems of imitative value. Placed beneath the final analysis, each ringeth as the coin in clarity or by its false tone it denotes the dross within.

Soul is as a mirror which reflecteth in speech its innate desire. The image revealed may be the angel's profile or the grotesque caricature of an evil aspect.

A mirror is that which receiveth the impression of the object placed before its surface. It enhanceth or it detracteth according to its workmanship. Thus is speech. It mirrors the pure thought or the adverse outpour of a perverted mind.

Upon the surface of the consciousness is imprinted each errant thought, there to remain until erased through the process of a comprehensive analysis. Whether the content enhance, or degrade, dependeth upon the mind's response to control.

Control is that through which order is maintained, this being the system through which supervision is established. Each soul who exists is subject to direct supervision. Soul believeth itself a free and independent agent. But the All-Seeing Eye sifteth each word apart, weighing its value upon the scales of pure intent.

The scales of justice sway from tolerance to prejudice. But ever doth the balance demand a final accounting ere it motionless stands, with equality established.

Equality is the state in which all are as one, like to like. This the Supreme Intelligence demandeth as the ultimate achievement.

Universality is that which embraceth all existent being. It is as a melting-pot of vast proportion in which is dissolved racial prejudice and the restraining wall of caste, to issue forth in the common mold of a united whole.

The mountain inspireth a sense of awe, its height commanding the respect which magnitude imposeth. Thus the high status of a selfless soul bringeth to humanity a glimpse of the height to which, in the course of evolution, each must ascend.

The desert extendeth beyond the physical vision. It seemeth an endless expanse of waste. Thus life appears to the soul whose thought-stream floweth in the channel of mediocre desire. Beyond the desert lieth the ocean's breadth, each tide being a revelation of the power which motivateth creation.

He who findeth the desert's sand as a morass in which he sinketh deeper with each step must of necessity develop the wings of the eagle. Thus thought soareth from the pit of despair to the heights of the sublime when the taper of Spirit, with increasing brilliancy, illumineth soul.

A star gleameth as a jewel in the dome of Paradise. It lureth from the height. Couldst thou trail it in the dust its glamour would be dimmed. Thus the soul whose vision looketh not to the heights but centereth its yearning on the depths.

Despair is the antithesis of hope. It leadeth soul to the blank wall of defeat, where through necessity it turneth to retrace its steps.

Memory bringeth joy or sorrow according to its mood. If it hold before mind the image of regret it worketh for good. If it giveth to desire the reflection of indulgence it must needs be disciplined, subject to soul's command for obedience.

Realization bringeth fruition, soul in fulfilment achieving the completement of its predominating desire. Whether this be a gem with which to adorn the consciousness, or a thorn which inflicts a corresponding pain, dependeth on the yearning delineated.

The diamond revealeth the ultimate of achievement, its prismic rays reflecting the radiant purity of the

Divine. First must it through cauterization be enhanced, its pristine state denoting the lack of culture. Thus soul, perchance innately pure, must through culture radiate the Divine, else its Light be buried beneath the exterior of a garment of reserve which revealeth not its intrinsic worth.

Purity is the depthless well in which soul is rinsed of its miscellaneous content. It disburseth that which savours of the mediocre, reflecting with crystal-clearness the Light of divine comprehension.

Comprehension embraceth the ability to understand. It revealeth the problem to its intricate depth, clarifying the mind that the logical aspect be revealed.

Stupidity denoteth the refusal of mind to the exacted obedience, mind through a perverse stubbornness accepting not the Law experience exemplifies.

Experience delineates the school in which each grade must be learned to completement. Many a soul returneth to study anew his forgotten lesson ere to him cometh comprehension of its purpose.

Life thrusts upon soul the necessity for growth. It teacheth the varying elements of joy, sorrow, hope, despair, disillusionment and fulfilment. He who repineth not but accepteth all maketh infinitely more brief the period involved.

Scandal is the robe with which infamy enwrappeth the guilty, or perchance the innocent member of society. It reduceth the recipient to the stature of the ant in the eye of public esteem. But the Law demandeth that the perpetrator in the ultimate receive in exact proportion the ignominy which he hath bestowed.

The Law which represents the karmic principle irrevocable is. It dealeth to each soul that which it hath earned regardless of consequence. None escapes that which he hath builded. The ascent may be made on the ladder of achievement. But if the lower bar delineate a weakness, the precipitation to the exact level of the error involved exacteth the building anew of the structure of life.

Man talketh glibly of wisdom, thinking it findeth its source in learning. But the Supreme Intelligence defineth wisdom thus: Wisdom lieth within the depths of the soul, which, in a profound humility, seeketh the portals of the Divine. There, inscribed upon the Eternal Records, lieth the source of wisdom. He who readeth therefrom hath first renounced selfish purpose. That which he readeth he giveth forth, with which to enrich the universal mind.

Oracle Seven

Man knoweth not the hour when the Grim Reaper wieldeth the scythe. If he await the summons with naught of his task undone it matters not. He who dallies leaveth that which he must perforce return to complete anew.

Retribution—man calleth the law of eternal consequence. But within the tenet exemplified, the thinking mind seeth the effect which ever lieth within the cause.

Each act beareth a consequence, be it of trivial or grave import. Thus soul, with the tools experience supplies, buildeth the foundation of its Temple of Thought.

He whose mortar lacks the lime of pure intent buildeth that which will crumble and collapse when the breath of adversity bloweth; within its content lieth the essence of distress.

Adversity denoteth the combined elements of pain and distress, be it of pecuniary or spiritual delineation. One partaketh of a privation which reacts on the physical life, the other of that which affecteth the Spirit.

Spirit urgeth soul to expression. As a breeze it bloweth with inconsequential import. Or, of cyclonic intensity, it driveth soul to the commitment of criminal proclivity.

Soul giveth acquiescence to Spirit's urge, thrusting upon mind compliance with its urgent dictum, which through mind expresseth in speech or act soul's desire.

He who governs not thought through unceasing control is as a merchant who selleth from his surplus that which denotes the integral part of dynamite.

Man grieves when Death knocketh at the portals of his heart. He crieth aloud in his bereavement, seeing not that which the unthinking mind calleth Death is in reality birth, who but masketh in disguise.

Birth is the means through which soul descendeth into physical manifestation. Rebirth is the multiple process. He who decrieth this law, refusing to absorb its content, is as a mute who striveth to speak, lacking the incentive for expression.

The mentally deficient lacketh the power of stabilized expression. Mind, motivating ceaselessly on the pivot of a deranged vision, taketh from the consciousness at random that which it distorts into wierd and grotesque form. Thus the Law worketh if of mind man maketh not an obedient servant.

The servant listeneth to the dictum demanding obedience. So each soul serveth at various periods of his evolutionary cycle. To thrust upon thy servitor the ignominy of a reproach lendeth strength to the element through which a similar service is rendered by the self. The law of rebirth operateth ceaselessly, forcing soul to rebuild each weakened strand in the fibre of its being.

Thy Father, the supreme and omnipotent God, decreeth all existent souls shall in the ultimate emerge on the basis of equality. When thou censurest thy brother who serves beneath thee look also to him who walketh in advance. Thus he seeth thyself.

Obedience is the predominating factor of service. He who learneth not to submerge the will in humility walketh with Pride, who proves a companion of ill-repute. Humility walketh with Love. Inseparable companions are these, the brothers of divinity.

Divinity compriseth the elements of the Divine, which are the seeds the Almighty God planteth within the garden of creation. To glimpse thy Father's handiwork in Nature's lavish bestowal is to bathe the soul in the fount of understanding, through which it emergeth as reborn.

The fount of joy within the depth of the soul effervesceth with bliss when soul through communion ascends to the high plane of divine conception. There lieth the panacea for pain when life teareth apart the tendrils of spiritual understanding.

Understanding provides the buffer which soul interposeth between the self and him who would wound with the harsh words of antagonistic disbelief. The rancour directed recoileth with the percussion of a blank cartridge, leaving but the smoke of defeated purpose as evidence of ill-intent.

The Ancient Wisdom embodies the elements of a profound interpretation. It giveth impetus to thought. But the soul which emergeth from an excursion therein must disrobe its being of illusion and mysticism, absorbing but the kernel of the nut and discarding the outer shell.

The nut comparable is to the soul which encaseth the Spirit. To extract from soul the divine spark leaves that which beareth not the semblance of life. To take from the outer shell the kernel leaveth but the husk of past endeavor.

Soul through consistent growth maketh an advance. If the course be impeded by an ulterior motive the backwash of thought teareth apart the supporting wall of the morale, giving entrance to the inflow of debris which soul hath accumulated in its diversified experience.

The flood overfloweth, bringing destruction and burying beneath its turbulent content the verdant soil. So the material instinct burieth beneath its waste the fertile garden of constructive effort. Long and devious the process through which soul disburseth this, the dregs of experience.

Experience teacheth soul the value of material aspiration. It reflecteth in the mirror of achievement that which soul hath garnered when the riches amassed, through a lifetime of effort, disappear as into the mist of the vaporous fog which blindeth the vision to that which lieth beyond.

The leper denoteth that which repels with the unclean. The moral leper contaminateth not only the adjacent individual but the mass-mind, within which he disburseth his unsavory thought.

Man tosseth the pebble within the placid pool, visioning with eager delight the varying ripples which outline its descent. Thus thought, projected within the ether, with incredible speed permeateth space. According to its quality is the area involved.

Holiness is that which partaketh of the Divine. It breathes of purity. With it the priest enwrappeth the supplicant who seeketh absolution. Before the Shrine of Eternal Being must each individual soul prostrate the self, receiving from the Supreme God the absolution of his sins.

Catholicism offers a haven to the soul which requireth the staff of collective worship. Within its tenets soul findeth the loaf with which to alleviate its hunger. The weakened link in the chain is that which requireth soul to, through the intermediary, seek the Divine. As the

arrow must soul through faith project the individual
self to the altar of divinity, paying in sacrifice the debt
incurred through selfish indulgence.

The Supreme God exacteth from the individual soul
the payment of that which it hath constructed of obligation. It payeth in full, balancing the Ledger of Life with
the debit and credit of its individual effort.

"Science" giveth to humanity that which enhanceth
thought. But within its tenets it demandeth soul accept
in its entirety the theory of the mind. Through control
of thought mind giveth obedience to Spirit's dictum
but through physical means the Master-Physician, thy
Father, createth the wherewithal for the alleviation of
physical pain.

There existeth naught of waste in the divine plan.
Each leaf, each tiny ant, filleth a necessary purpose.
Whyfore thinkest thou the Supreme and Infinite Mind
giveth, through that which Nature bestows, the vast
waste which the abstinence of creed's dictum demands?
Each straw which whirleth in the breeze hath borne the
seed evolution requires. Each lark which trilleth in a
fervor of joy hath brought to completion its purpose.
Each soul which expresseth in thought the divine pattern
delineates its preordained motive. Whyfore thinkest
thou Nature wastes the tools through which thy Father
worketh?

The mind which accepteth all, denying none, exemplifies the Universal. Thus co-operative, all that which
exists dependeth on a corresponding atom for completion. Creed giveth the ladder through which soul maketh the ascent to freedom, each integral part delineating
an active principle. He who stoppeth, refusing to make

the ascent, provideth a barrier to his brother, who passeth not the restricting wall.

Drink thou, Beloved, from the fount which quencheth thy thirst. But tarry not when thou cravest the additional draught. Ascend to the broad road of multiple thought that thy soul, cramped, becometh not crystallized in that which it hath outgrown.

He who clingeth to the outgrown garment of a restricted creed weareth that whose usefulness is completed. Discard the fetters which bind, releasing soul to the broader understanding its growth demands.

Oracle Eight

The Divine Mind embraceth all existent souls. To extract the illuminating spark therefrom, merging into the essence of selfless being, delineates the process to which humanity in the ultimate must evolve.

Evolution provideth the attributes through which soul selfless becomes. As in a mighty cauldron of experience doth soul motivate, until through the momentum attained it casteth off the weakness characteristic thereof to, through purity, function as a selfless being.

Man scoffeth at the delineation of the karmic principle, thrusting the blade of derision therein. But when Adversity knocketh at the portals of the mind, breaking to atoms the resistance, as a babe he accepteth the discipline inflicted.

The miser counteth his gold in an ecstasy of joy. He seeth not the soul shriveled as the autumn leaf. Thus is the materialistic mind, which thrusts upon soul the famine of a spiritual deficiency.

Spirituality produces the fertile soil which receiveth the seeds of divinity. It enricheth alike the individual soul and humanity. For the aroma of its fragrance permeateth the mass-mind.

Elementary the knowledge of biblical delineation. It weaveth with the threads of fantasy the fabric of a poetic dream. To extract its divine element must the seeking mind sift through the sieve of a comprehensive analysis its content.

The Ancient Wisdom embraceth the combined content of countless philosophies. Blended into the Wine of Life, each element denotes a characteristic flavor. According to the individual taste must the goblet of elixir be drained. To supplant the juice of the vintage with the sparkling champagne of profundity, is as to nourish the babe with the full content of the adult's repast.

Deficiency delineateth the lack of content. Excess produceth an over-supply. To combine these, the factors of necessity, is equal to subtracting from luxury the waste which depletes penury.

The mass-mind receptive is to the inflow of thought. Through the will of the Supreme Intelligence is interjected therein when necessity demands the incense of the spiritual essence, to, through its potent impetus, stimulate the content. To extract the gold from the predominating dross is to produce a leaden mass. To likewise reverse the process is to produce a richer mixture. Thus the Supreme Chemist administers to humanity that which supplies its current need.

Chemistry delineateth the process of analytical demonstration. It addeth and it subtracteth as necessity demands. So soul passeth through the chemicalization process, that through the interjection of the tincture of pain it become in the ultimate the purified substance.

Geography giveth to the mind the ability to, in thought, vision a certain locality. Mind accepteth with avidity the area designated for exploration. When the spiritual analysis requireth the acceptance of the etheric antithesis of being, mind in opposition demandeth tangible evidence thereof. How then analyze the wind which cometh from the Unseen; the lightning which findeth its birth in space; the rain which floweth from the dome of Nature's infinitude? How dissect the mind which operateth through the agency of thought if it, through instinctive rebellion, refute the source of its inception?

The flower which enhances with its ethereal beauty revealeth to the spiritual vision, upon each radiant petal, the image of the Divine. To the mass-consciousness must man turn in reverence for that which motivateth its being.

The mass-consciousness giveth to the mineral, vegetable and the animal kingdoms the wherewithal for motivation. It embraceth, it sustaineth and it, when dissolution ensues, accepteth the integral principles, through the law of rebirth producing its replica, with each element advanced in the scale of evolutionary delineation.

The united kingdom intrigues with its intricate delineation. It giveth to the adolescent mind the insurmountable barrier of an impenetrable wall beyond which thought findeth not entrance. To the thinking mind it lendeth the substance with which to erect the foundation for the understanding, which alone giveth evidence of growth.

The divine conception confuseth with its impenetrable mystery. That which findeth its source in divinity defieth unless the spiritual analysis layeth bare its content. Conceived through the will of the Omnipotent God, it exemplifieth the process employed to bring to fruition the individual soul.

The embryo, be it of whatsoever nature, embraceth the divine principle. It revealeth the mystery of birth and of death, each giving to the element involved the opportunity for growth. The acorn becometh through the law of rebirth the mighty oak. The babe evolves into the adult. And the adolescent through evolution becometh the intellectual. Canst thou differentiate the principle involved?

Mathematics lendeth to mind the necessary exercise for growth. It stimulateth thought, making facile and plastic the surface. To, through concentration, manipulate its content is akin to, through muscular exercise, training the recalcitrant muscles to obedience.

Mind is the sieve through which thought poureth. According to the content doth it give response. It may through receptivity drain faultlessly the substance. Or, through inefficiency, may the sieve denote an obstructing element. Through control of thought is a state of efficiency maintained.

The consciousness is as a parchment of immeasurable breadth, which receiveth the imprint of thought. He who writeth thereon with the indelible ink of perverse thought constructs that which will prove as a blister which refusal lends to treatment, inflicting on mind a corresponding anguish.

Anguish giveth to soul the impetus for an intensive analysis. It proddeth the consciousness, demanding a disbursing of its perverse content.

Joy bestoweth tranquillity, the repose through which soul produceth the masterpiece of a rare loveliness. It buildeth with the tools of divinity that which liveth forever in the annals of thought.

The canvas which beareth the divine image liveth throughout the ages. That which man buildeth with the tools of a perverse desire is as an ill odor which through dissolution leaveth in its wake a sense of profound disgust.

Eternity compriseth that which imperishable is.

There soul through service exemplifieth the Divine Will. The adolescent seeth this state as the Nirvana of suspended effort. The advanced soul knoweth immortality denotes the process through which soul serveth the Christic Being in a fervor of joy.

The Christic principle embraceth the elements of selfless being. It partakes of the divine attributes. It giveth all and asketh naught. It perpetuateth love whose root denotes tolerance and compassion blended. It findeth in its supreme example the Living Christ who, in celestial being, exemplifieth that love which depthless, immeasurable and all-encompassing is.

Oracle Nine

Consciousness serveth soul as its imperishable store-house of knowledge. It giveth to thought the where-withal for expression. Thus mind through affiliation responds to Spirit's urge.

Mind submitteth to the inflow of thought, lending support to active delineation. It giveth to soul the op-portunity to express in speech or act its predominating desire. The servant of soul, it through affiliation sup-porteth thought. Brain supplieth mind with the where-withal for active delineation of thought. It, through the multiple nerve-centers, forceth the physical organ-ism to responsive measure.

The physical organism denoteth the supreme creation of the Omnipotent God. Intricate, marvelous in con-struction, it through the multiple nerve-centers submits to the urge of desire, giving to mind the autocracy of control.

Spirit, soul, mind and body embrace the active factors of being, spanning the breadth from spiritual delinea-tion to the process of physical being. Evolution pro-videth the bridge which lendeth support to the inter-change of activities.

Experience proveth the harsh task-master who, through diversified opportunity, giveth to soul the power of expansion. It thrusts upon soul the tincture of pain and it reveals the heights of bliss. In reality it, through discipline, teacheth the invaluable lesson of self-control.

Will-power is that through which soul forceth mind to obedience. If desire be concentrated upon that which uplifts it worketh for good. If it delineate a perverse tendency it teareth apart the morale. When a foe of evil it is a force of supreme magnitude. Desire giveth to will-power the necessary channel for activity.

Desire thrusteth upon soul the necessity for expression. It findeth its birth in thought, which is in reality Spirit's urge forcing upon soul the necessity for activity. Soul through lethargy refuseth mind the opportunity for diversified experience. Spirit, the motivating agent, being of divine origin, through the impetus of thought provideth the urge for expression. Diversified experience it is through which soul taketh cognizance of its motivating power. To curb desire through the process of thought-control, forcing it within the channel of constructive effort, buildeth stronger the morale.

Life thrusteth upon soul the goblet of fulfilment. It drinketh of the bitter draught of defeat or it draineth the elixir of joy. Whatsoever the mixture, it, through the alchemy of emotion, teacheth the lesson soul hath earned.

Soul, being of divine origin, enwrappeth Spirit, which is its animating genius. Spirit partaketh of the Divine, finding its source in the cosmic exemplification of the Supreme Will, which in universal expression createth all that exists. To subtract from soul the infinite spark leaveth but the outer shell which encases. To from Spirit take its enveloping robe is to bare that which is its illuminating element.

Cosmic the interpretation of the universal principle, it being the power of supreme magnitude through which the Almighty God expresseth His omnipotent will. In a power whose magnitude is immeasurable it giveth that which sustains the universe. It permeateth the atom, be it of whatsoever denomination, alone giving the wherewithal for being. Cosmic the universal principle, which is in reality the Omnipotent Will.

Time denoteth the process through which mind apportions to activity the exact dimension. It existeth as a tangible expression of thought. The etheric universe knoweth neither time nor space. The Divine Will giveth to soul the innate strength for continuity of effort. The physical organism denoteth the necessity for repose, that its multiple nerve-centers through relaxation support the rehabilitative process. Cosmic the inflow through which revitalization is executed.

The atom provideth the integral and fractional segment for analysis. Infinitesimal its intrinsic substance when through separative issue it standeth apart; of supreme magnitude when through cohesion, augmented by the cosmic essence, it denoteth bulk. From the crystallized atom to the mountainous principle is spanned the process evolution provideth for amalgamation.

Infinitesimal the tiny insect which through activity delineateth the supervision of the mass-consciousness, which provides the element of initiative which motivates action. Through evolution the tiny ant becometh the giant beast. But first must the law of rebirth with unfailing precision regulate the individual span of creature existence.

The mass-consciousness embraceth the supervision under which the various kingdoms motivate. Mineral, vegetable, animal—each alike giveth obedience to law. The human alone possesseth the attribute of the soul, which provides the incentive for individual effort. In reality the Divine Will operateth through mass-supervision, that to each kingdom be given the wherewithal for consistent growth.

Supervision compriseth the intricate system through which control is established. It embraceth all existent atoms, organic and inorganic, carnate and discarnate. Naught escapes the espionage which delineates the Law. The bee worketh beneath the mass-consciousness, which limits its scope of activity. The beast provideth the necessary adjunct to the progress of the soul expressing through the physical habiliment. Each supplieth its superior with the necessary element for growth. Each functions beneath the irrevocable law of control, deviating not from that which evolution demandeth as progress.

Elemental the principle which the propagative instinct delineateth. The mystery of creative being, it defieth dissection by the lay-mind. Through the ovum the seed becometh the mature, be it in whatsoever kingdom; desire being the predominating element which motivateth action, the result being the propagating of the species.

The propagating instinct findeth birth in desire, which is soul through expression delineating Spirit's urge. Herein lieth the mystery of creative life. Spirit, being of divine origin, it through the cosmic principle receiveth the impetus for active demonstration of the Omnipotent Will.

Cosmic the interpretation of universal being, in reality the exemplification of the will of the holy and supreme Deity, God.

Oracle Ten

The cosmic delineation of being provideth the hypothesis for extensive analysis. Flowing from the source of the Omnipotent Will, it giveth to creation the wherewithal for manifestation. He who accepteth the Law, through which universal control is established, seeth in the cosmic essence the sustaining force which motivates the universe.

Soul through innumerable rebirths functions on the various planes of interpretative delineation. It, in etheric or spiritual antithesis, contrasts with the physical analysis. Each succeeding birth furthers the evolutionary process through which growth is assured.

Progress is essential in the scheme of evolution. Consistent must be the unfoldment of the individual soul, as in a flower each petal unfolding to the love-force which permeates its integral being; love being the predominating and supreme force which motivates.

The creative instinct findeth its impulse in the sphere of celestial being. Generated through control, its analysis lendeth itself to the cosmic interpretation, this being the supreme power through which the Omnipotent God furthers creation.

Man and beast respond in like measure to the propagative instinct, this being the foundation of the law of rebirth. Propinquity lendeth support. Through Nature doth the vegetable kingdom respond, in renewed verdure exemplifying the divine law.

Nature through a diversity of means giveth to creation the necessary adjuncts for progress. Through spring the law of rebirth bringeth to the physical universe the

opportunity for gestation. Through autumn the somnolescence of a profound repose indicateth the process
of disintegration. The adolescent mind seeth in the
demise of summer the reverse of birth. The thinking
mind glimpseth the eternal spring towards which each
autumn bringeth closer the varying elements involved.

The mighty oak through its bare and majestic presence commandeth respect. Man seeth in it the strength
which sustains. The soul whose spirituality draweth as
a magnet the weaker example, resembleth the oak. The
delicacy of adolescence hath been replaced with the
rugged grandeur of a supreme repose.

Adolescence giveth to soul the period through which
in diversified experience soul drinketh from the goblet
of varied content. It sippeth the elixir of the gods and it
draineth the dregs of bitterness and disillusionment.
Distilled, the brew indicateth the draught through
which soul is purged of its innate and predominating
weakness.

Maturity denoteth the stage of progress in which soul
through innumerable rebirths hath cast aside the robe
of materialism, replacing it with the mantle of divine
understanding.

The alloy of bitterness is as a lubricant. It blendeth
with the oil of self-esteem, eradicating from soul the
predominating satisfaction which maketh it brittle and
adamant.

Universality is that which embraceth all and denieth
none. It compriseth the elements of Christic being.
Founded on love, its roots extend throughout the soil
of civilization, its tendrils embracing with compassionate instinct all existent philosophies and creeds. Even

as the loaf findeth its fundamental principle within the grain of wheat, so each philosophy findeth in its basic foundation the grain of truth. Soul through concentrative analysis must pluck from the text its element of truth, discarding the illusion and glamour enwrapping its substance as the adornment of a decadent era.

Truth findeth its source in the Divine. It permeateth the universal thought-stream, lending the substance which facilitates its current. Subtracted, the flowing waters would become stagnant and turbid of content. Amplified, the sparkling depths suggest the crystal-clearness of the effervescing spring.

The Ancient Wisdom findeth its source in the field of extensive and profound thought. It revealeth the divine concept of being, lending itself not to material exploitation. The soul whose innate purity demandeth the manna with which to alleviate its hunger, within the source of the Divine turneth for enlightenment. First must selfish purpose become non-existent, the seeker accepting the bestowal, not for the individual, but for the common good. Service it is which is thus exemplified.

The ancient teaching of biblical delineation revealeth the source of creation, the collaborators thereof giving to the generation in question the foundation for innumerable creeds. Civilization through progress demandeth the Wine of Life be clarified, a broader interpretation replacing the ancient text, that, combined, thought turn instinctively to the motivating force, acknowledging the supreme and omnipotent Power which sustaineth being. The compassion, the love, the depthless understanding which centuries ago were exemplified in the supreme Master of the ages, revealeth the source of the current interpretation. From the celestial heights the

Christic Presence bestoweth the attribute through which the crucifixion taketh place. The individual soul must through the identical process crucify the self upon the cross of divine comprehension, this being the ultimate of all.

Oracle Eleven

Transfiguration denoteth the illumination through which soul perceiveth the essence of the Divine. It discardeth error as a barrier to progress, building with the tools of pure intent its imperishable store-house of thought.

Illumination partaketh of the process through which soul glimpseth in varying content the Divine. The light of understanding receiveth birth, through which the divine elements of compassion and tolerance become manifest.

The soul which gropeth in the darkness of a disbelief seeth not the Divine Mind, having erected a wall of prejudice through which the divine ray penetrateth not. Soul through sorrow, with a corresponding disillusionment, must give birth to the yearning which fosters the seeking instinct.

The adolescent prattles of the tinsel with which soul enwrappeth the being. It is the lure through which experience beckons, desire being the predominating urge which impels soul to activity. Experience in reality holdeth the mirror in which soul glimpseth Illusion. Scintillating its image until through adversity the blurred replica is revealed as but a mask for despair.

The intellectual hath attained the power of reason. This denoteth the advanced stage. Soul partaketh of the process of extensive analysis. If the spiritual impetus provide the undertone of the soul's harmonic rhythm the Portals of Wisdom open wide, permitting entrance to the plane genius delineates. But if the indifference of a profound self-esteem maketh of soul a glacier of reserve the intellectual ray is dulled, as it is deflected from the blank wall of scientific investigation.

The intellectual ray in reality revealeth the plane of profound attainment. Soul through its innate strength projecteth thought to the source of its inception. Immeasurably enriched its content. If the mind be receptive to guidance the heights attained denote the acme of achievement. The genius thus receiveth the impulse through which is created the sublime masterpiece of art. If the cold light of ascetic sufficiency permeate the mind the divine ray, deflected, but casts its shadow over the soul, the near-attainment delineating the presence of the divine element which eludes the seeker, who grasps not the content but the shadow of the sublime.

Conversion is the term by which the lay-mind designateth the rebirth of thought. At the psychological moment indicated as applicable, the ray of divine comprehension illumineth soul, cleansing with its healing propensity. Thus the uplift giveth an increased strength through which are disbursed the shackles of error which fetter. The light of comprehension illumineth with its clear radiance. Subject to rancour and derision, soul must through initiative rise above this which is inflicted, realizing that the scoffer will in the course of time become the penitent.

Rebirth delineateth the process through which soul maketh the advance. It is in reality the quickening of the tempo of the spiritual pulse through which an ascent is made to a higher plane of consciousness. Through transition is provided the means of a comprehensive analysis, soul reviewing in endless continuity the sequence of past experience until through satiation, with a corresponding anguish, it relinquishes that which formeth its predominating weakness, in supplication approaching the source of divine healing.

The rebirth, through which the soul in physical delineation experiences the metamorphosis, partaketh of the elements which its etheric counterpart undergoeth on the plane of spiritual interpretation. Soul receiveth that which evolution designates as applicable at the exact period its receptivity permits.

The divine instinct impels soul on its journey through the Cosmos. It giveth to soul the impetus which fosters growth. Its momentum augmenting unfoldment is tempered to the exact speed which experience demands, desire being the agent which through temptation tests the innate strength according to the current need.

The realm of spiritual interpretation lureth with its mystery of being. The adolescent seeketh in phenomena to probe its content. Akin to playing with disaster is this process in its perverse experimentation. Innumerable the souls of astral proclivity who seek to establish contact with the physical universe. Through the medium of thought is this accomplished, ofttimes a subtle influence becoming manifest which, if of an evil character, leadeth to an increased desire for the perverse. Like added to like denoteth an increase of desire. This in reality is but casting additional fuel to the fire.

The term *astral* designates the spiritual antithesis of the physical universe. Thus function the souls who, through the interchangeable law of being, denote the discarnate analysis. The immortal status lieth in advance, this being the ultimate of all. Intervening, various planes of consciousness denote the ascent to be accomplished. To realize that soul with unerring precision changeth from spiritual to physical, from discarnate to carnate exemplification of being, is to understand the law through which communion is established, thought being the imperishable attribute which maketh feasible the contact.

Consciousness is that which denoteth the stage of evolution in which soul functions. It is the receptacle of thought. It receiveth the mind's content, which is disbursed with unfailing precision. It denoteth the exact plane on which mind functions, the understanding revealing the period of growth. The consciousness in reality is the store-house in which soul deposits the fruits of experience. When necessity demands its content is subject to a comprehensive analysis, the inventory necessitating the elimination of that which may be designated as waste. Imperishable, it lendeth soul the power of expression.

According to the spiritual strength manifest doth soul express desire. It centereth its yearning on the mediocre or on the sublime. If strength be deficient, an unattained quality, soul through perverse expression denoteth its inefficiency. Thus soul trendeth the path evolution provides: from infancy to maturity, from adolescence to profundity.

The elementary revealeth the primary grade of attainment. The intellectual denoteth the profound. Thus soul, through its manifesting agent, thought, expresseth its innate strength. He who prattles idly is as the shallow stream. He who weigheth his words through control is as the silent but swiftly flowing current. The thought-stream denoteth soul's grade of attainment.

Oracle Twelve

The aspirant to initiateship knoweth naught of selfish purpose. Soul, illumined by the divine spark, giveth allegiance to the Supreme Deity, seeking in selfless service to exemplify the Divine Will. Casting aside the fetters of materialism, it, through its innate yearning, projects the self to the source of the Divine, there receiving the impetus for increased effort. The path of the initiate, through its steep and narrow length, delineates the supreme sacrifice the crucifixion of the self exemplifies.

Selflessness giveth to soul the advantage of service. It, through affiliation with other souls of like status, in a fervor of joy giveth of its all. Compassionate, understanding, it seeketh to alleviate human ills, through the healing propensity demonstrating its unity with the Divine Mind, of which it formeth a fractional part. Thus the invisible Brothers of Humanity serve the Christic Being in whatsoever sphere necessity demands as applicable to effort, guidance being the predominating factor, embracing the element of thrusting upon soul the experience through which in the ultimate purity is assured.

The material mind refutes the existence of a Universal Brotherhood which in spiritual analysis serveth humanity. It accepts but that which the physical vision embraceth. To, through faith project soul to the source of the Divine, barring prejudice which is as a barrier to illumination, is to receive that which forever banishes the darkness of a disbelief. The spiritual vision encompasses the realm of divine interpretation and the light of understanding provides the basis for the theoretical calculation which embraceth alike the physical universe and its antithesis, the spiritual.

In etheric substance existeth the spiritual universe, it being in reality that of which the physical is the replica. Changeless, eternal, it reflects the divine creation. Here, through Christic leadership, function the white-robed Brothers of Humanity, this being the ultimate of all existent souls. It exemplifieth the selfless state of being, soul through spiritual evolution having made the ascent through the varying creative planes of consciousness to the celestial status, that which bestows the divine prerogative of serving in active affiliation the predominating head, the Christic Being; *brotherhood* being the tie which uniteth; service being the keynote of harmonic affiliation. Discarded that which partisanship embodies. Racial discord, creed—all merge in the divine comprehension which permeateth being. Thus serve the Brothers of Humanity, their vast number augmented by an increasing number of souls whose ascent to the supernal heights delineates the fitness for the ultimate of service. To realize that the individual soul beneath the law of constant supervision functions; that each thought which flickers across the surface of the mind leaveth a corresponding imprint within the consciousness, there to be weighed eventually on the scales of a comprehensive analysis, indicates the futility of believing that soul freed is of the responsibility of error. The individual soul payeth each debt it contracts, be it of whatsoever denomination.

The Christic Being whose all-pervading love permeateth the universe, whose depthless compassion indicative is of the supreme attribute, from the supernal heights in Living Thought serveth humanity. From the crucifixion which the Supreme Deity imposed that the example of selflessness be exemplified, that throughout the eternal ages be made manifest the law of crucifixion, is to be glimpsed the light eternal. The Master Jesus, who through physical delineation descended to teach humanity the elements of sacrifice, through Living Thought sendeth forth this message, teaching the universal principle, instilling within the seeking soul the necessity for sacrifice; through the healing propensity solacing the lame, the halt, the soul-weary aspirant. Herein lieth the antidote for suffering. Here is outlined the course each soul must in the ultimate embrace. Through the elimination of selfish desire, the castigation of the mind, the adherence to the Law which brotherhood imposeth, the living within the Law, giving the all but taking not—these are the essentials through which soul casteth aside the tinsel of the mind, replacing it with the pure gold of spiritual attainment.

The Christic principle is that through which soul in subservience prostrates the self before the Supreme Intelligence. It weareth the garment of a profound humility, for within the aura of the Holy Presence its weakness becometh apparent and the desire is given birth for a closer unity with the Divine Mind. It seeketh through the example bestowed to emulate the Divine Will. The peace which pervades soul giveth the essence of a supreme content. Thus soul, prostrate, recognizeth the source of its being, accepting the ultimatum the Divine Will imposeth, knowing naught but the ever-increasing desire for service. Soul through affiliation with kindred souls is given an increased strength. The love which uniteth unselfish is, giving of its all. It, through active demonstration, provideth the all-sustaining power of universal control. Cosmic the delineation. For the supreme force which permeateth being is that which unites, sustains, motivates, the holy and omnipotent Will being thus expressed. The scoffer turneth from the wisdom herein bestowed, in derision. But the law of evolution irrevocably transmutes from the physical to the spiritual, from the spiritual to the physical. Thus the alternate law of rebirth operateth. He who in the adolescence, the immaturity, of thought scoffs, will in the metamorphosis of the ultimate in penitence seek the source of the Divine. Thus worketh the law of compassion. The weaker member must be enwrapped with the understanding of a divine comprehension. As the babe must be viewed his halting efforts, his inability to accept the spiritual manna which the advanced, the mature, soul demandeth. Compassion denoteth the essence of healing love enwrapping the afflicted, the weaker, soul.

Sacrifice demandeth of soul obedience, it being in reality the submergence of the individual will within the Divine. Soul accepteth all, rebelling not. If it be of physical or mental pain, disability of the physical organism, through which soul findeth the ultimate of experience, or an unrest so depthless, so profound that it partaketh of despair—whatsoever the condition imposed, within it lieth the cauterization through which acceptance is given birth. It is the element of sacrifice which teacheth obedience. None are exempt. If a transient period be given for the purpose of stabilization accept joyfully, realizing that this but precedes the additional testing of the mettle.

Jesus the Nazarene exemplified the law of supreme sacrifice. The soul through innate strength forced the mind, the body, to obedience. It, through acceptance of the Divine Will, ascended the cross, there to in poignant anguish reveal the depth of human woe. The clerical mind turneth in reverence to this example of sacrifice. It pointeth the way to the Cross as the course of the individual soul. But unless enlightened it visions not the varying and innumerable existences through which soul must in diversified experience crucify desire to attain the ultimate. The Cross is the eternal emblem which each soul must surmount, until in selfless delineation it lifteth its weight, transcending the physical to, in selfless being, serve Him who bestowed its symbol in the depthless understanding which motivates love.

Oracle Thirteen

He who liveth within the Law, accepting its tenets, knoweth neither fear nor superstition. For the predominating faith which sustains maketh soul impervious to the hardship which mind inflicts when, through lack of stabilization, its strength is deficient. Mind it is which worketh a hardship on soul. For through habit it refusal gives to obedience. To subjugate the mind through the process of thought-control is to facilitate progress.

The ancient philosophies through superstition impose a variety of hardship upon the seeker of truth. Through the process of incantation the sense-centers lend themselves to a disturbance which, if not controlled through the power of will, terminate the seeker's exploration in the occult by immersing soul in a perverse habit, which through its debilitating effect on the morale seriously weakens resistance. If continued, it, through obsession, which is in reality adverse astral control, may result in the unbalancing of reason. It may in a torpor react on mind, thrusting upon the individual a pronounced lethargy of thought. Through organic disability it may impair the physical organism. Will-power proveth the agent through which control is established. To project soul in meditation to the source of the Divine is to receive the inflow of the healing essence of love.

The law of rebirth confuseth with its suggestion of mystery. It in reality provideth the means through which evolution is fostered, giving to soul the interchange of vehicles, alternating from spiritual to physical antithesis. To reject this, the irrevocable law of eternal significance, is to subtract from evolution the wheel on which it rotates. Rebirth alone supplieth soul with the process experience provides. It giveth the exact impetus to thought, the medium through which soul expresses. Thought, the silent monitor, impelled by Spirit's urge, thrusts upon mind, the motivating agent, the necessity for co-operation. It, through brain, the physical organ, manipulates the nerve-centers which motivate the muscles through which bodily energy is made manifest, the vocal organs lending themselves to the articulation which the lay-mind designates as speech. An intricate and marvelous exemplification of the supreme art of the Creator, this, the co-operative process of soul, mind and body.

Mind, which findeth its origin in soul's insistence for expression, formeth the sieve through which thought is poured within the consciousness. Its external surface receiveth the thought, which desire, promulgated by Spirit, impels therein. Man demandeth the reason for the origin of thought of a perverse nature. Thought is the means through which speech or act is fostered. Thus is diversified experience promulgated, soul through experience manifesting the various emotions which are as the tempest when anger or sorrow disturb the mind. Peace and joy lend a compensating tranquillity which is as the calm sea, comparable to the tide-racked ocean. Soul, the enveloping robe of Spirit, through its opaque tone or its translucent quality, revealeth the stage of evolution in which it functions.

Groping within the darkness of a spiritual disbelief is the soul which, through a perverse tendency, refuteth the consoling essence of love. It relieth on its own strength, glimpsing not the divine ray which sustaineth the fibre of its inmost being. Created through the divine instinct, motivated through the cosmic essence of love, sustained through that which love exemplifies, it turneth from choice to the darkness of a disbelief. To such a soul must the enlightened extend the compassion which seeth the weakness with naught but pity which, fused with love, enwraps. The babe knoweth not the laws beneath which the parent motivates. Such a soul, through ignorance manifesting the evil proclivity, is as a babe in evolution. Condemn not, but by example, by firmness which through the absence of harshness commands obedience, demonstrate control. The silent stream runneth not in an adverse direction. Its innate strength impels it through the channel which enlightenment provides. But the turbulent brook babbles noisily as it bruiseth its content against the various obstacles placed in its path, and which of necessity must be surmounted. The mighty ocean of Eternity receiveth in the ultimate the varying tributaries, offering the harbor of security when the tempestuous course is completed.

Eternity provideth an inexhaustible subject for analysis. It embraceth all that exists, for it knoweth neither the beginning nor the end of creation. The supreme and mighty God, the magnitude of whose power lendeth itself not to comprehension, through control manifests the divine prerogative. The universe illimitable is. The individual soul as but one mosaic in the divine pattern of the infinitude must, through comprehension of immensity, experience a profound humility. The tiny ant, which laboriously constructs its habitation, which man relentlessly destroyeth, a necessary adjunct is to evolution. The individual soul in like manner lendeth itself as necessary to the eternal scheme of continuity. The atom, through dissection beneath the microscopic analysis, infinitesimal is; but in unity it establishes the bulk of which the physical universe is composed. The soul likewise formeth an integral part of the Great

Whole. To comprehend the significance of this fact is to, in humility, approach the Shrine of Universal Being. The depthless love through which creation is fostered, the profound concern evidenced for each individual creature, illuminative is of that through which the divine spark findeth its inception.

The atom which lendeth the scientific mind the basis for analysis denotes the etheric compound. Permeated by the cosmic essence, which is the elixir of universal being, the cohesive tendency is fostered through which amalgamation becometh an active factor. Thus is established bulk content. Thus doth the planetary orb evolve from the gaseous formation into the solidity of a substantial planet, which giveth to the incoming generation the necessary habitation. The law of equality governs progress. The incipient ego findeth its creation in the divine spark which, through the process of absorption, enfolded within the cellular membrane of the mass-consciousness, becometh the soul which through evolution, fostered by innumerable rebirths, demonstrates the physical delineation of the etheric analysis. Long and devious the process, equality supplying the exact habitation necessary for the stage of evolution involved. The atom through cohesive tendency, fostered by the cosmic inflow, provideth the basis for atomical construction, lending itself to the process of amalgamation.

Cosmic the universe and all that it embraces, this being the force through which the Supreme Will operateth. Man speaketh of this supreme force as the Omnipotent God or Jehovah, accepting according to his understanding the interpretation thereof. The orthodox mind prefereth to accept the biblical delineation of the universe in its literal sense, refuting the spiritual interpretation. A strange complex this, for each recurrent generation denoteth an advance, the mind accepting with alacrity each additional appliance science provides with which to facilitate progress. The clerical mind, through an instinctive reserve, erects the barrier of a prejudicial belief, clinging with an impregnable tenacity to the practical delineation of a teaching bestowed two thousand years ago through the auspices of various agents. A masterpiece of supreme beauty, the Bible delineates the birth of thought according to the ancient doctrine of those who operated in that generation. With each additional translation it has suffered, its ancient text being amplified until its present delineation offers much that varies from fact.

The purpose of this manuscript is to supply the foundation of a philosophy which offers to the thinking mind the hypothesis for a universal conception. It teacheth that the supreme God commandeth the soul's profound adoration; that to His chosen mediator, Jesus the Christ, be given the homage which accepts the Christic principle as the ultimate, the supreme ideal on which to pattern. It accepteth the Christic teaching, the life of Jesus; emulating the supreme sacrifice as the gleaming light which illumines the path. The Cross symbolic is of that on which each soul must crucify the self. This teaching, through its simplicity, its purity, delineates the Christic Being who from the superlative heights extendeth that love, that compassion, that divine tenderness, of which in ages past the prophets foretold. Universality embraceth all and denieth none.

Oracle Fourteen

The Divine Mind embraceth all that exists, in tangible and intangible being. It is in reality the love which emanates from the source of the Almighty God, which through its healing propensity enfolds with a peace whose depth is immeasurable. The soul who through faith seeketh the source of its inception is lifted above the fret the physical universe imposeth, freed from that which harasses, at oneness with the Supreme Power which alone giveth alleviation from distress. Meditation provides the necessary means for attunement. Within the Silence, which is in reality the vast Infinitude, doth soul find surcease from that which perplexes, which torments with its burden of care. The Divine Mind, all-encompassing, all-embracing, is therefore the love through which the Supreme Presence is made manifest.

Meditation is the soul's haven. It provideth the means through which soul is made receptive to the healing inflow. Through various attitudes doth the aspirant seek the solace necessary for sustenance. The Universal Teaching delineates the process as one which requires the obedience of mind to the dictum of silence so profound that the errant thought finds not entrance therein. The physical organism must through a complete relaxation co-operate with mind in the silencing of thought. Soul in supplication approaches the Holy Presence through the Beloved Mediator, beseeching the healing inflow. Thus is communion established. The soul who through adverse propensity must needs erect a protecting barrier against astral intervention may, through the building in thought-form of the Cross, establish that which protection gives. The Cross, the divine symbol of the supreme sacrifice, builded in the reverence of prayer, is as a shield which soul erects. Its significance, its spiritual essence manifesting strength, alike make of it an insurmountable barrier. Soul, in relaxation, unless through purification immune to interference, findeth in the process that which protection gives. Meditation is the course through which soul seeketh a unity with the Divine Mind for the purpose of an increased strength with which to foster evolution.

The spiritual universe is an enigma which the material mind findeth extremely difficult to comprehend. It automatically demandeth tangible proof of the object under scrutiny. This attitude of disbelief, of antagonism, erects a barrier through which soul is immune to the inflow of the spiritual essence, it being deflected by the crystallized surface mind presents. The spiritual universe delineates the discarnate antithesis of carnate manifestation. The soul, freed of the physical organism, merges not with oblivion but, superlatively active, centers its activities on whatsoever plane of consciousness its evolutionary period provides as adaptable to its needs. It, in etheric or spiritual form, motivates. Its inherent weakness, its desires, are ever-present factors, until through comprehension of the futility of error it renounceth the barrier to growth, centering its yearning on the attainment of the spiritual. To realize that soul imperishable is, that it alternates between the varying planes of physical and spiritual analysis, is to in a measure comprehend the supreme wisdom through which incipient being is perpetuated. Upon the physical plane are innumerable and varying degrees of consciousness. The adolescent, the mediocre, the advanced, the intellectual—all delineate various stages of growth. What lieth between their differing degrees of understanding? Rebirth alone provideth the means of analysis; rebirth through which soul descends at alternate periods, ripe for the experience the vicissitudes of the flesh provide.

Rebirth, which the ancient philosophy terms *reincarnation,* is the connecting link through which soul in advance riseth to a higher plane of consciousness, a broader understanding. Dissolution of the physical tie is an essential factor. The spiritual unity imperishable is, the love which the companionate unity delineates, in which the divine elements are harmonious. That which is based on the magnetic affinity, which the sex impulse exemplifies, is as the ember which alone suggests the flame which has burned to extinction. Thus the perverse, the physical desire, is cauterized through that which disillusionment provides, satiation thrusting upon soul the necessity for a comprehensive analysis. The propagating of the species delineates the means through which rebirth is fostered. But the racial instinct taketh not into consideration this, the holy significance. It, through propinquity, motivated by the sex urge, accepteth parenthood as a corresponding necessity. Experience then, thrusts upon the individual soul the elixir of bliss and the depth of despair. But beyond the haze which blurs the physical vision exists, in its radiant unfoldment, the spiritual antithesis of being.

The consciousness through which soul cometh into an awareness of the fourth dimension, the realm of spiritual analysis, provides the target for adverse and ofttimes malicious criticism. It offers to the lay-mind a profound mystery, impenetrable unless to soul hath come the conviction that the spiritual analysis exists. Soul through open-mindedness, approaching the Shrine of Universal Being, casteth aside the barrier of prejudicial belief. If its sensitivity permit, the soul being receptive, with

naught to interfere, it senses the Invisible Presence, the
Guiding Force. So may be designated the white-robed
Brothers who serve humanity in the joy of selfless being.
It may through the inflow of thought touch the source
of creative instinct, demonstrating that which genius
delineates. Thus the masterpiece, be it of whatsoever
nature. It may with the spiritual vision glimpse the glory
of the celestial dawn; may for a brief moment experience
the rapture of a unity therewith. Soul must through
purity establish its fitness for the reward it craves ere it
is admitted to the realm of the Divine.

Innumerable planes of consciousness separate the soul
which functions in physical delineation from the realm
of immortal continuity. To attempt to establish communion unless the thought-stream be purged of selfish
purpose is to, in deficient strength, reach but the plane
of the soul's yearning. If it center on material aspiration
it of necessity reaches but the astral antithesis. Ever
must the seeker bear in mind the law of equality. Soul
riseth not above its inherent longing. The perverse functions on the level its desire imposes, be it in astral or
physical activity. Dangerous the method spiritualism
delineates, leading ofttimes to obsession, which is in
reality control through magnetic affinity. Thus is crime
delineated, being traced directly to astral dominion.
Insanity provideth an enigma. Mind, through the temporary or permanent separation from soul, pivots on the
rod of its predominating desire. To astral proclivity
may be traced innumerable deflections from the path
normalcy provides. Unless faith sustain the soul in its
yearning for communion, pure and unselfish purpose
dominating thought, the result will lack the harmonious
conception which is the reward when through unity soul
is encompassed within the Divine.

Thought, through which soul expresses its instinctive desire, in a diversity of means impels action. It may in mediocre or perverse analysis characterize the individual. It may through evil import leave a scar on the public mind. It may through mediocre attainment debase the current thought-stream. Whatever its quality, it expresses the stage of evolution in which soul functions. In opposite measure, it may create a symbol of divine interpretation; a strain of melody of a haunting sweetness; a canvas of surpassing loveliness. Thought, the voice of soul, it is which in active effort delineates the soul's innate weakness or strength. Spiritual leaders thus make appearance when a crisis in humanity demands the impetus of a spiritual awakening. As the gloom of a darkened night by imperceptible degrees giveth acquiescence to the manifestation of dawn, thus the spiritual rebirth delineates the advance in consciousness of the generation in question. Pivoting on the axis of Time, civilization lendeth itself to a reversal when through adversity comprehension of its innate weakness becometh apparent. Love is the motivating factor which, through the process of cauterization, demands an inventory be taken of the soul's waste or treasure.

Oracle Fifteen

Thought delineates the process through which soul expresseth desire. It is the intangible element which lendeth itself not to dissection through the analytical method. Thought then is the motivating agent of mind, the autocrat which thrusts upon mind the necessity for compliance. Of varying strata may be this, the soul's agent, its substance dependent on the exact stage of evolution in which the soul in question functions. It may from the mediocre to the intellectual run the gamut of experience, each era being comparable to a separate and distinct plane of consciousness. Only thus may be analyzed the discrepancy between that which adolescence and that which profundity delineates. The thought-stream floweth through innumerable channels of emotion. Perverse, uplifting—whatever it be, it expresses the predominating desire which motivates soul, this being the relentless urge through which soul experiences the vicissitudes of the physical existence.

Emotional, the senses respond to whatsoever experience provides. The lure of romance may thrust upon soul the heights of bliss or its antithesis, the depths of despair. It may provide a dawn of indescribable loveliness when soul unfoldeth as the petals of the rose, this being the spiritual essence of love, the magnetic and imperishable tie which unites the companionate souls throughout Eternity. It may through the false glow of passion sweep soul through a torrent of perverse indulgence, weakening the fibre of the morale and tearing to shreds the resistance, which is but another pseudonym for will-power. One strengthens, enhancing soul, clarifying the mind, making it receptive to the spiritual impetus. The opposite is retrogressive in trend, debilitating in effect and causing the thought-stream to carry the debris of a profound disillusionment, with its accompanying element, satiation. Soul seeketh the level of its innate desire.

The emotions lend themselves to analysis only through the path of diversified desire, this being the urge which impels soul in its quest of experience. Anger is the expression of frustrated purpose. It giveth to soul the demoralizing effect of loss of self-control. The will-power proveth insufficient to sustain thought on the high level of a stabilized basis. Greed delineates the yearning to accumulate material possessions, soul in a fervor of desire reaching forth, striving to wrest from whatsoever source manifests supply an excess portion of its content. Barren and devoid of compassion the soul racked by this, the predominating factor of selfish purpose. Hatred provides the element in which soul in retaliatory measure seeketh to wound its object, vengeance being the aftermath. Various crimes in hatred find their inception. It is as a blight which, through its virulent effect, bringeth to soul the consequence of a critical disturbance. Through successive existences may soul in physical disability bear the fruits of the incipient seed, until through a comprehension of its predominating weakness, through the agency of intense suffering, it eradicates the seed of discord.

Turning to the uplifting factors of the emotional element, we find compassion, this being the flower of spirituality. It enwrappeth with the healing essence of love. It provides the ladder through which soul maketh the ascent to the superlative state of being, which delineates the selfless status. It is the active principle which the Christic Being sought to instill within humanity when through the crucifixion He established the supreme example of sacrifice. The true significance of this, the crucifixion, eludes the mind which seeketh not the Light of understanding. The Cross symbolic is of that upon which each existent soul must in the ultimate crucify the self; the subordination of the individual to the Divine Will; the elimination of that which is destructive, which tends to weaken the morale. No act is devoid of consequence. No spoken word lacks its corresponding result. It must of necessity be uplifting or demoralizing. It must be constructive or destructive. The careful builder weigheth each thought, which reflects in speech or act. Thus doth the foundation of the Temple of Thought denote no faulty masonry.

Love giveth to soul the power of motivation. It is that which provides the wherewithal for expansion. It is the radiant Light which the divine element within produces, the Light which cometh from but one source, the Supreme Intelligence, thus demonstrating His omnipotent power. Love then, is the Divine Will which operateth that to soul be given illumination through its integral element, Spirit. Divine the origin of the infinitesimal spark which motivateth being, the active agent of the Supreme Intelligence. Cosmic the interpretation. For thus is the universal conception. To comprehend the operation of this, the Supreme Will; to realize that the cosmic interpretation alone sustaineth analysis; that each atomical unit is motivated by the cosmic essence— this formeth the hypothesis of a true analysis of fundamental creation.

Through the element of the cosmic essence is creation perpetuated, each atom responding according to the stage of evolution it represents. The Spirit being the incipient ego, it is the nucleus of the soul. Through divine ordination each recurrent generation of incipient souls issues forth from the realm of inceptive creation, with exact precision delineating the law of rebirth to, through the course of eons, become a generation with the power of individual thought. The mass-consciousness giveth to each individual soul in its inceptive stage of being the haven. Enveloping the incipient spark, it provideth the soul-structure, absorption being the process through which the cellular construction lendeth itself to the separative issue. Marvelous the meticulous system involved, from incipient being to the maturity of the intellectual attainment outlining the cycle evolution provides for fulfilment of the Law, rebirth being the ever-active factor of growth.

Soul, through its translucent tone, denoteth the superlative attainment, its radiance being the illumination of the divine element which forms its nucleus, it in reality being the purification through which soul hath cast aside its inherent, its innate, weakness. With each succeeding rebirth, if growth be consistent, an advance is made to a correspondingly higher plane of consciousness. With each advance the enveloping aura, which is in reality the outer garment of soul, delineates a clearer tone, a more vibrant quality. The divine element with a more pronounced intensity illumines its enshrouding robe. This alone giveth to soul its radiant and brilliant tone. It is the Light within which is the active principle of the Divine. To enumerate the varying colors with which the aura lendeth itself to change must the element of thought be interjected. Thought, which is the voiceless language of the soul, transformeth according to the emotion expressed the outer garment. When through selflessness soul hath become innately pure, the absence of ulterior motive eliminates the opaque tones which are characteristic of the stages of evolution when soul still functions within that which the evolutionary cycle provides. The Immortal reflects the high attributes of love, understanding, compassion, these producing the aura of pure loveliness, exemplifying the soul's yearning to serve.

Oracle Sixteen

The creative instinct findeth its impetus in the Divine. Fostered through the Omnipotent Will, it reflects the element of supreme achievement. The lay-mind speaketh of inspiration, vaguely understanding its true significance. The advanced soul realizeth that through but one source alone cometh that which thrills with its potent beauty. To realize that the soul which createth a divine masterpiece is one who through direct contact hath established a unity with the realm of interpretative thought, is to comprehend in a minor degree the law which governs evolution. This unity may be through a conscious awareness of its source. Or subconsciously soul *en rapport* may transcribe the content of its yearning. Soul is given that which it hath earned. If through an innate purity it has demonstrated its worthiness to an advance, the creative impulse motivateth the effort for achievement.

Harmony produceth a state of profound tranquillity, this being the condition in which soul is pervaded by a peace through which it visions humanity with compassion. The fret of the physical universe is deflected, leaving not the imprint upon mind which results in an unrest, a pronounced discomfort. The peace which permeates induces soul to renewed effort. It subconsciously strives for a closer unity with the Divine, instinctively gravitating toward the source of its being, the love-essence being the magnet which draws.

Subtle and insidious the effect of flattery upon the soul. It, through the inflation of the self-esteem, giveth to soul a sense of false security. Vanity formeth a generous measure of the compound. Soul, enhanced by the rosy glamour of success, faileth to differentiate between the true and the false. It relies on its own strength, which at the crucial moment proveth insufficient. Thus is pricked by the needle of adversity the multi-colored bubble of a profound self-satisfaction. Flattery weareth the garb of the sophisticate, flaunting the draperies of Illusion.

Illusion provideth the necessity for scanning with profound concern the garb of the soul which masqueradeth as friendship. As a wanton, Illusion lureth with the semblance of reality.

Friendship embraceth the element of devotion, which gives unstintingly, demanding naught in return, sacrifice being the predominating trait. The adolescent soul protesteth its eligibility to this sacred attribute, understanding not the nature of its creation. It findeth its birth in love. It liveth in service. And it endureth eternally.

The reservoir of thought, which is in reality the Universal Mind, unlimited, immeasurable, is. It affordeth the supply from which soul draweth when through evolution it hath discarded selfish purpose, centering its yearning on the desire for service. It is as a depthless spring which effervesceth with an ever-increasing brilliancy, its clear waters reflecting the image of the Divine. The thinking mind delineateth this process as the manifestation of genius, which is but another interpretation of inspiration.

The necessary qualification for the achieving of the steep ascent to communion, for that oneness with the Divine Mind by which thought is released through the inspirational inflow, is the yearning to enrich humanity, to give freely of the supply, with naught of desire for remuneration. Fame, public acclaim, recognition, homage from the world at large, form no part of the recipient's desire, for the soul *en rapport* with the Divine instinctively turneth from these, the worldly attributes, consciously or subconsciously placing the true valuation thereon. The golden crown with which fame adorneth the brow of the conquerer taketh the tone of the tarnished metal, denoting the dross content when through adulation soul loseth the power to discriminate. Flattery and adulation are in reality the acid test applied that the innate strength be measured on the scales of divine comprehension.

The laws which govern soul's progress delineate the necessity for the control of thought. Soul functions through its own volition, making choice of the path its fancy dictates as applicable to its present need. This path may lead through a diversified experience or it may trend the byway of an extended detour, which through the course of an entire existence may thrust upon soul the monotony of a colorless era. Poverty may pave the path with the cold stones of want and privation. A physical infirmity may lower the resistance, thrusting upon soul the dregs of acute suffering. The mind may through derangement endure a temporary period of mental anguish. These various conditions delineate the necessity for a profound self-analysis. They in reality delineate the necessity for a reversal of thought. Compassionate must be the regard with which this stage of evolution is visioned, for it thrusts upon the object the accumulated debt which must be discharged before the weight is relieved.

Karmic the obligation which soul accepteth when, through suffering and hardship, its course is deviated from the tranquil existence which denotes a state of well-being. Irrevocable the law of cause and effect, which delineates the working of the karmic principle. The material mind accepteth the law of happenstance, living within its tenets. It refuseth recognition of the all-embracing supervision which through control outlines the path of experience, thrusting upon soul the necessity of choice of that which is advantageous to growth. The material mind inclineth to the theory that soul operateth as a free agent; that it oweth to none that which conflicts with free choice. Why then is soul powerless to halt the avalanche of woe which descends upon it at the psychological moment apportioned as that in which it reverse its course? It, through a succession of calamities, of mishaps, marvels that the tide of adversity with relentless force sweeps from beneath the supports of material advantage. Thus is the individual soul castigated and thus, when necessity demandeth, is a race or a generation cauterized. The law of cause and effect is in reality the hand of love which brushes from the consciousness, with tender concern, the debris of wasted effort.

Love is that which motivateth being. It provides the force which alone sustaineth soul. It delineates the depthless, the all-embracing element which, of divine origin, is in reality the Omnipotent Will expressed. From the source of the Supreme Intelligence cometh that which surpasses the understanding of the mind, whose limitation permitteth not a true comprehension of its import. It embraceth the elements of understanding, of sacrifice, of submission. It partakes of a devotion which tirelessly gives, withholding naught. These are the attributes of love, that which soul exemplifies as its rightful heritage. The divine spark, which is its nucleus, is as a mirror which when purity is attained reflects the glory of the perfect whole.

Oracle Seventeen

The Universal Mind embraceth the content of thought. It delineates the supply from which is drawn the incipient seed. Soul through the process purification supplies denoteth its fitness to, through communion, establish a unity therewith.

The Divine Mind delineateth the essence of love, the force which through its healing propensity motivates the individual soul. According to its receptivity is it enriched. The vessel, be it of whatsoever denomination, holdeth but the content its inherent bulk delineates. Thus the individual soul; its receptivity dependeth upon the depth of the understanding through which soul expresses its innate yearning.

The universal principle is that which exemplifies the Christic teaching. It outlines the path the individual soul must trend from incipient being to the ultimate attainment.

The Christic Being, who from the supernal heights demonstrates the process of control, reflecting through the selflessness of the supreme attainment the Holy Will, demandeth that each soul must through the purification process eradicate selfish desire. This is the impediment which restricts soul on its evolutionary course.

Through indulgence is desire manifest, the yearning delineating the necessity for gratification. The advanced soul regardeth the weakness of indulgence as a necessary grade in the school of experience, its purpose being to, through the satiation of a profound disillusionment, bring to soul a comprehension of the futility of error. The weakness, be it of whatsoever nature, lendeth itself to control through but one process, that which care, accompanied by disillusionment, supplies. Thus soul glimpseth the tarnished strand which sustains not the light of the close scrutiny which bares its inmost content. The gold must needs be refined before it becometh the perfect metal.

The cultural instinct which alone acts as an incentive to effort urgeth soul to the completement of the objective to be gained. The law of disparity, which thrusts upon the individual the comparative process, lendeth stimulus to effort. Within the inequality of universal being lieth a purpose. Each soul seeth in advance a soul of correspondingly higher attainment. Through example the desire is given birth for a similar achievement.

Inequality provideth an enigma to the adolescent mind. Through the socialistic instinct it striveth to wrest from the predominating head the power invested. It in fantastic effort attempts by insidious doctrine, which breathes of selfish purpose, to instill within the mass-mind the adverse impulse which is of destructive measure. To tear from the individual the material benefit which is the result of laborious effort would be to take from humanity the incentive for exploitation. Within example lieth the urge for increased activity.

The selfless status reflecteth the ultimate which each soul must emulate. Through diversified existence is the purification process promulgated; each existence indicating, through the reversal of thought, a step in advance.

The Golden Rule of ancient delineation holdeth within its tenets the irrevocable law of universal control. It is in reality the backbone of the religious principle. If man bestoweth in thought, which motivates speech and act, but that which his innate desire prompts as applicable to himself, he taketh not from his neighbor that which he prizes; he inflicteth not that which wounds. He giveth but that which uplifts, which heals. Here is exemplified the depth of love. To wound is to delineate the desire for retaliatory measure. To manifest but the yearning to heal precludes the possibility of injury.

The material mind in selfish purpose striveth to extract from the world at large that which satisfies his greedy instinct. Ofttimes he destroyeth ruthlessly to accomplish the fruition of his plan. The peace of mind of an individual is his most priceless possession. He who taketh this, the soul's treasure, contracts a debt of supreme magnitude.

Theft is practiced in innumerable channels. But the act first findeth birth in desire, which through the process of thought exacts obedience of mind. The injury to the object lieth in the reaction, which inflicts a pronounced mental distress. It may affect the pecuniary status, working a privation through which the individual undergoeth a reversal of circumstance. This of necessity worketh a hardship on mind, which in unceasing complaint disburses its burden of woe on the companionate souls which experience hath provided in close proximity. It may induce a despair in which the suicidal tendency becometh manifest. It may through adverse influence, as when leadership is involved, through example shock a race or a nation. Whatever the hardship, the culprit must in like mental anguish obviate his debt.

The Golden Precept in a brief summary teacheth the futility of error. To, in concentrative effort, analyze its potential quality, applying it to the self when temptation thrusts upon soul the necessity for choice, is to immeasurably strengthen the morale.

When through the crucifixion Jesus the Supreme Master ascended to Christhood, He gave to humanity the teaching through which was to be established a Universal Brotherhood. He sought to instill within humanity the foundation for a philosophy of love; that which would preclude hatred and racial antagonism, caste, the restricting barrier of creed. Humanity repudiated His teaching in its entirety, accepting the example of the crucifixion in varying degrees of analysis. The orthodox mind in literal interpretation of the Bible deleteth much of its spiritual content.

The profound philosophies expose not the kernel of the nut. The soul, adaptable, through its individual stage of evolution must laboriously, painstakingly, scrutinize each enwrapping fold, extracting in its pristine beauty the underlying truth. The mind, through an intensive analysis must penetrate the depth of the subject involved. The student of the occult, through an exhaustive process of concentration, eventually arrives at the fount of understanding. But his thirst remaineth unquenched until through the intricate process of comprehensive analysis he hath mastered the instinctive desire for self-indulgence. The conquering of self, the elimination of desire, the subservience of the individual will to the Supreme Will—these are the essentials of the process of purification.

The orthodox mind scanneth the pages of the ancient masterpiece, the Bible, accepting literally its content. Barely brushing the surface in thought, it penetrateth not the intricate depth which must be probed before enlightenment becometh apparent.

Truth formeth the foundation of all existent philosophies. But the soul which seeks in immersion therein to alleviate its spiritual hunger must train the mind not merely to brush the outer surface in thought but, in an intensive analysis, to seek within the content the pure gold, which alone satisfieth.

Christhood delineateth the supreme achievement. Soul becometh the purified substance. Being of divine origin, the infinitesimal spark which formeth the nucleus of soul must through illumination dispel the gloom which the evolutionary period embraces. It must by imperceptible degrees lend itself to the love-force which motivateth and sustaineth being. Through the varying existences, each bestowing the fruits of experience, it with an increasing brilliancy reflects the divine ray which animates. Soul in reality is as a bud which, exposed to the sun of love, slowly responds, unfolding its petals into the perfect flower. Thus is the divine pattern exemplified.

The incipient spark is as the seed implanted within the soil of experience, through alternating existences in spiritual and physical antithesis to, through unfoldment, mature into the perfected and divine element. Soul in reality traverseth the karmic cycle. It reacheth in the ultimate the accomplished circle, the dross extracted and the pure gold of the purified substance delineating the Divine.

Oracle Eighteen

The Christic attribute denoteth the selfless state of being. Soul, innately pure, functions as the divine element, immortality having been the portal through which soul entered to, in spiritual delineation, exemplify the Law. The requisites for selflessness are those which comprise an understanding so depthless, so all-embracing, that it reflects the divine element, love being the motivating impulse. Through the Christic attribute the weakness, the idiosyncrasies of the flesh, are regarded with compassionate concern; the yearning to solace, to shorten the evolutionary cycle, being that through which supervision is promoted.

Service denoteth the means through which soul maketh the ascent. It is that which the Supreme Intelligence exacts on whatsoever plane of consciousness the Immortal functions, the yearning being proportionate to the service bestowed. Ever in advance lieth that to which soul aspireth.

The material mind which centers its longing on the aspiration to which the physical universe lendeth support, comprehends not the instinct through which the free soul motivates. The spiritual universe savours of unreality, a myth which the mind thus burdened deemeth unworthy of serious consideration. Evolution, with its varying fields of activity, provides the means through which the reversal of thought taketh place, bringing an ever-growing awareness of the proximity of the Unseen.

The spiritual delineation of being produceth an enigma of vast proportion. Soul, being of etheric composition, motivated by the divine element which we designate as Spirit, of its own volition gravitates with increasing endeavor towards the source of its being, soul being as the steel drawn by the magnet of love, that love which the Supreme Being exemplifieth, through which His power is expressed. To deny the existence of the Unseen is as to attempt to draw the camel through the needle's eye. For the multiple forces through which Nature motivates defy analysis by physical means. Space, which illimitable, immeasurable is, revealeth the source of the Divine. There, in etheric delineation, functions the spiritual analysis of being. Space embraceth all; universal the scope.

Space, which the lay-mind defineth as an unexplorable area, in reality composeth the universal principle. In eternal continuity the constellatory orbs function; each, through that which its individual stage of evolution provides, functioning with the precision the Divine Will affords; each, in the course designated as applicable to progress, to receive a generation of incipient souls. Eons comprise the time involved, in which the ego through the building of the soul-structure evolves into the individual soul, thus to, through innumerable rebirths, become a free agent. Through the spiritual hypothesis alone is it possible to give a plausible explanation of the origin of the soul which, through the auspices of the mind, expresses in physical delineation.

Permeating space and each separate atom thereof, we find the etheric compound. Intangible, incomprehensible, it defieth analysis by physical means. Cosmic the interpretation, as is all that exists. It revealeth the means through which evolution is fostered. It in reality giveth to the atom the buoyancy through which the cohesive instinct is fostered. Permeated by the cosmic essence, the etheric compound lendeth itself to the divine instinct, gravitation being sustained. The etheric compound it is which, through inter-penetration, lendeth to the atom its constructive formation.

The lay-mind speaketh of the atom as an infinitesimal particle. It thus delineates the construction of matter. Atom to atom, the cohesive instinct promulgated by the cosmic inflow, amalgamation taketh place, bulk quantity becoming thus established. Vibrant, each particle through its resilient quality giveth support to another atom of corresponding growth, equality being the ever-present factor. The cellular construction denoteth the supreme art of the Great Jehovah. The mass-consciousness which formeth the protective issue beneath which the mineral, vegetable and animal kingdoms function affords the initial construction of the cell. Ovular, it, when evolution maketh feasible, gives to the ego, the incipient spark, the receptacle through which the soul structure is formed, absorption being the intricate process involved, promulgated by the ever-present cosmic essence, which is the life-producing and life-sustaining force.

The inceptive realm, which in reality supplieth the source of the creation of the individual soul, formeth the base of the hypothesis of the creative instinct. There, through the operation of the Supreme Will, the individual soul findeth being. Through the separative issue the divine spark, cosmic in derivation, is implanted within the receptive folds of the mass-consciousness, there through indeterminable eons of time to repose, exemplifying the formative process. Cosmic the love-force which motivateth being. Through its magnified intensity is the separative issue imposed, the infinitesimal and divine element with automatic precision being deposited in its enveloping cell, to become through the evolutionary process the individual soul. Thus is the mystery of creative life revealed, that a true delineation replace the obsolete and erroneous impressions existent.

The propagating instinct revealeth the means through which rebirth is fostered, Nature being that through which the Divine Will is expressed. Instilled within the object is the creative urge, the functioning organs responding to the impetus supplied. The vegetable, the animal, kingdoms obey the dictum of Nature with unfailing and systematic regularity. The physical organism of the human likewise delineateth obedience to the law imposed. Nature represents the guise through which the Divine Will expresseth, that the law of rebirth be fostered.

Nature, which provides a lavish display of beauty, giveth to the physical universe the wherewithal for sustenance. It supplieth in generous measure that which gratifies the senses, which lendeth support to thought. To delete from the physical universe the varying color-tones which enhance would be to create a drab and dreary panorama. The eye would through monotony become dull and listless. The mind would delineate a barren field, having within its content naught on which to draw for the embellishment of art, of literature. To subtract from the physical universe color would be to immeasurably impoverish humanity.

Color denoteth the harmonic affiliation of tone. Of vibratory measure, it receptive is to the cosmic inflow, responding in like measure. It denoteth an ethereal delicacy, a fragile loveliness. It blendeth its varying tones into the intensified depth through which contrast is established. Innumerable the moods which Nature exemplifies. The sun, which is the mother-principle of whatsoever planetary orb is represented, lendeth the warmth which brings to fruition the element involved. It, when Nature demands, blighteth with its too-ardent rays. It, through atmospheric control, deals a lavish display of beauty. Or it parcheth, brushing the vegetable kingdom as with a mighty stroke, that its power be manifest. Color is the invisible, intangible, spiritual essence which in physical antithesis delighteth the senses of man.

The material mind accepteth the existence of a Supreme Deity with apprehensive concern. It regardeth a God of wrath, of retribution; or it accepteth an exemplification of love, depthless, profound. According to its understanding is the delineation represented. The orthodox mind believeth a solitary existence is the total experience of soul, it through the Nirvana of a sustained peace functioning when life's fret hath subsided and soul passeth to its eternal reward. Satisfying this interpretation when mind, through the fog of adolescence, glimpseth not the spiritual significance. To repose in an eternal state of bliss would be as a blight to spirituality. Through growth, unfoldment, an ever-increasing unity with the Divine Mind, doth soul respond with a corresponding bliss. He who walketh with love as an inseparable companion hath reached the stage of growth where peace is an established factor, a peace so profound, so all-embracing, that the service exemplified knoweth naught to mar. Humanity, with its innate weakness, is revealed as a necessary stage of being, it representing a school in which soul through sacrifice and endurance learneth the lesson of self-control. It inspireth a compassion which is all-embracing, through which service is joyfully exemplified. Thus the invisible Brothers of Humanity serve, delineating the Christic principle beneath the direct supervision of the Supreme Master, Jesus the Christ.

Oracle Nineteen

From the supernal heights is control established, that supervision which in its intricate mechanism is incomprehensible to the mind which is subject to countless disturbances, the fret of the physical existence thrusting upon soul an endless variety of hardship in which the endurance is strained to the limital degree. The mind, which operative is through affiliation with the brain, hath not the power to comprehend the spiritual antithesis of being except in a minor degree. Its area is of necessity limited to that which the physical universe affords for exploration. The physical vision embraceth but that which the immediate area offers. The mental area is likewise limited to the scope thought covers in retrospection. The brain which demonstrates obedience to the dictum mind imposeth, if taxed to a degree incompatible with its innate strength, will through a pronounced nervous reaction set up an opposition. According to its understanding doth each soul accept the current interpretation of the spiritual antithesis of being.

Control, through which the universal principle is governed, is established through a supervision so intricate, so vast, that but a fractional part is released that humanity glimpse the supreme art of the Omnipotent God. Control in reality is the exemplification of the Divine Will, vested in an authority whose magnitude is unfathomable. The Beloved Son, the Christ, through the mediatorship imposed demonstrates the Supreme Will. Thus between humanity and the Omnipotent God mediates the Christ in a compassion, a love, which are depthless, who may be termed in a profound reverence the Elder Brother. The supplicant maketh the soul's obeisance to the Great Father, acknowledging His

power, His love, His supreme art. But to the Son doth
the seeking mind turn in reverence. For herein is vested
the healing essence which solaces, uplifts and sustains
the supplicant who approaches the holy shrine in humility of spirit. To turn to the Elder Brother when the
vicissitudes of the physical existence fret, to in the Silence beseech the Divine Audience, is to emerge immeasurably enriched, the compensating peace testifying
to the unity established with the Divine Mind.

The United Brotherhood of Jesus delineates that vast
group of selfless souls who have attained the immortal
status, having made the ascent through the varying
planes of consciousness to the attainment of the Christ-
consciousness, that state of being which precludes the
attribute of aught but selflessness. The celestial attainment giveth to soul the privilege of, in direct communion, serving the Master. It, through association with
kindred souls of like status, serveth beneath the Supreme
Mediatorship humanity, the compassionate instinct for
alleviation being the predominating characteristic. In
whatsoever field of activity, in whatsoever capacity
the Divine Will ordaineth, serve these, the invisible
Brothers. The *Guiding Force* they may well be termed.
For the individual soul, be it in whatsoever stage of
evolution, findeth but that which its immediate need
demonstrates as the necessary experience. It may be the
distress of a profound unrest or the tranquil calm of a
peaceful era. But back of and motivating the individual
soul is the ever-present guidance of the Invisible.

Jesus the Christ personifies the supreme attainment.
It is to the Christic Being the individual must turn when
through stress of sorrow, of pain, of disillusionment, so
profound it bruises the soul. Herein lieth the source of

the healing power. The orthodox mind demandeth the reason for the mediatorship thus exemplified. The God whose love, whose wrath, form the opposite exposition in various creeds, ruleth the universe. Through His power, whose magnitude lendeth itself not to measurement, is control established. That which lieth beyond the supernal realm, where serve the Master Minds of celestial being, is veiled. Thought permitteth not entrance thereto in current delineation. But, representing the Supreme Intelligence, reflecting His power, His love, is the Christ who, through innumerable channels, exerciseth control. Life, be it in whatsoever field of activity, is subject to control. This is the irrevocable law of karmic delineation, a superior or commanding agent limiting the soul's activity. In the clerical field the organization denoteth a predominating head. The financial mart is governed through rule and order. The governmental chief exacteth obedience from a nation. The law of control likewise regulateth the supernal or etheric realm, lending that which impels obedience. The Christ thus exemplifieth the Father's will, through His mediation establishing the universal control which embraceth creation.

Creation embraceth a wide field of activity. It is in reality the universal principle delineated, the creative impulse permeating the individual soul; likewise the floral attribute, the beast, all grades of matter respond to this, the universal impetus, through the urge of the procreative instinct furthering creation. To create is to form, to build, to, from the essence of the Unknown, bring into being whatsoever the object exemplified. The impulse which for convenience we designate the creative instinct, must of necessity motivate effort. From but one source cometh this, the divine impulse. It is the active element which is promulgated through the Supreme Will, which in cosmic delineation maketh known its power. Cosmic the inflow; in varying degrees of magnitude, this is the nucleus of the creative instinct which motivates creation.

The cosmic universe is that which delineates the creation of the Supreme Intelligence. It embraceth all that exists in spiritual or physical delineation, in tangible or intangible form. It embraceth alike the vast army of souls, carnate and discarnate; the planetary system in spiritual or physical analysis. For all existent objects must first in spiritual essence be formed before the replica in physical expression is established. Thus is embraced the universal principle. Governing the universe through united effort, under the direct supervision of the Master Jesus, serve the white-robed Brothers of Humanity.

Oracle Twenty

The law of rebirth torments the lay-mind, which findeth in its tenets that which tends to disrupt the calm of a disbelief. It repels through suggestion of the severance of the love-tie which uniteth in physical being the souls involved. Within this unity lieth a purpose of profound proportion. The recalcitrant soul respondeth but to the tincture of pain as administered through the auspices of a companionate soul. It, through sorrow, through the separation death, preferably called transition, imposeth, is brought into a realization of that which spirituality represents. For, through the depth of the soul's anguish is given birth the yearning for enlightenment; the soul seeking in the darkness of sorrow's gloom for that which lends a promise of continuity. Thus soul in yearning seeketh the source of Light. Disillusionment, despair, physical infirmity—all these are the wedges through which soul is separated from its inherent lethargy, its antagonistic disbelief. It is in reality the torch which the Guiding Force flashes before the spiritual vision, that it take cognizance of the Divine. The law of rebirth affordeth soul the joy, the bliss, of a reunion in spiritual being when the uniting element is based on the spiritual affiliation, exemplifying the eternal thread of love.

Eternity is a term which lendeth the support of the imperishable interpretation. The material mind, which measures its content through the hypothesis of physical means, finds itself enmeshed within the limitation which the restriction imposeth. It must needs resort to the calculation of the metrical system in order to apportion the exact limit involved. To realize that the physical existence is but one brief chapter in the book of eternal continuity, that preceding and following after the existence in question lieth Eternity, is to in part adapt the mind to the law of rebirth.

The creation of the individual soul lieth within the eons past but the divine element which illumines, the Spirit, eternal is. It partaketh of the Great Whole, being as an infinitesimal grain of sand bordering the Sea of Life. As such it, through the law of proportion, filleth a purpose. It lendeth support as a fractional part. The divine pattern must through its completeness denote the perfected whole. Thus the individual soul through affiliation formeth a link in the chain of perpetual being.

Spirituality embraceth the elements of the Divine. It partaketh of the supreme accomplishment, being the essence through which the soul is motivated. It is in reality the cosmic interpretation of being, the part of soul which, purified, reflecteth the Spirit's radiance. Spirit, being the illuminative spark of divinity, must needs through a diversified experience penetrate the soul's structure, disbursing the opaque essence and instilling the translucent quality which denotes a unity with the Divine Mind. The aura it is which reflects the stage of evolution manifest. It may through its narrow width denote the opaque dullness of the mind closed to spiritual interpretation and acceptance. Or it may through its encircling radiance reveal the soul in a close unity with the Divine.

The dilemma of the orthodox mind lieth in its inability to enlarge its scope of thought. The restricting barrier of creed offers a limitation. Thought, confined to the limit mind imposes, becometh stale. It lacks the liberty, the freedom, that a diversified training bestows. The diet if confined to a narrow margin, by its very monotony impinges on the appetite, dulling its craving. The mind likewise respondeth to the restriction of thought, becoming cramped, by its lack of versatility wearying the associate who strives vainly to enlarge its content. Soul, mind, body, the three organisms which Spirit motivates, unremittingly demand nourishment in diversified quality, relaxation, impetus for fresh effort derived from that which variety affords. The universal course is to, through diversified interests in varying fields of thought, provide mind with a healthful diet for sustenance.

Philanthrophy is the field in which soul striveth to alleviate the common woe. It may through pecuniary assistance seek to solace the needy. It may through the spiritual manna supply the soul with the needed nourishment. In various channels is this, the divine instinct, delineated. To realize that compassion is the predominating factor animating soul is to, in a measure, support. Through the disbursement of surplus wealth doth the favored soul make an advance. Wealth is the test imposed in which soul's strength is measured. If selfish purpose predominate, soul will cling to its surplus content, embellishing in wasteful appurtenance the excess supply. This but delineates the karmic law of reversal when soul in poverty will return to, in physical being, learn anew the lesson encompassed. Love, not fear, must prompt soul to share with its needy brother the excess supply.

Integrity is that in which soul denoteth the innate honesty which delineates strength. It hath chosen the path of constructive effort and deviates not from its narrow margin. Principle is the name by which this attribute receiveth recognition.

Purity delineateth the spirituality existent in the individual soul. The thought-stream floweth through the channel of spiritual understanding, instinctively rejecting that which savors of the unclean. It is the status which soul hath attained when the evolutionary cycle denoteth the near-approach to completion.

The karmic cycle giveth a field for extensive exploration. It delineates the course of the individual soul from incipient being to the maturity of the intellectual capacity which reflects the spiritual impetus of thought. The karmic law is the designation for the governing principle beneath which soul functions on its evolutionary path, the irrevocable law of cause and effect which apportions to soul that which it hath earned, the compensating issue of joy or despair. He who recognizes the intricate working of this, the law of control, regulates his efforts, diverting them from the channel of self-indulgence, soul instinctively turning to the source of its being for the unfailing guidance supplied. To realize that naught is happenstance, that within each thought, each act, lieth a corresponding result, is to limit soul's activities.

The cause it is which reflects the effect. Thought, which is the urge of Spirit thrusting upon soul the necessity for expression, motivateth mind, which demands obedience from the brain, through operation of the nerve-centers producing activity in speech or act. Within this brief delineation lieth the functioning power of the divine impetus which impels Spirit to response.

Oracle Twenty-One

The senses comprise the ability through which soul expresses in physical means its desire. Through the optical delineation soul taketh cognizance of the physical universe. It thus tabulates the surrounding landscape, the near objects which form the wherewithal for habit. It appraiseth the article in question, forming an estimate of its value. Thus is sight demonstrated.

To appraise an article, giving to it an estimate of its true value is it necessary through manipulation to establish its content. Here the sense of touch is a necessary adjunct. Thus the fingers, exceedingly delicate through the training habit employs, examine the texture, determining its basic formation. When through examination an object intrigues, the individual, exercising the sense of smell, inhales its fragrance. Thus he placeth a more complete valuation on the rose, whose ethereal beauty is enhanced immeasurably by the delicate aroma which permeates its fragile loveliness. Here are combined the operation of the three senses: sight, scent, and touch.

The ability to hear is that through which the conversational impetus is furthered. In *repartee* the individuals concerned, through an interchange of opinion, test each other's ability for thought, the mind responding with alacrity to the stimulus imposed in comparative effort. The sense of hearing delineates the means through which soul in a fervor of joy responds to the harmony of sound, the strain of melody lulling to a deep tranquillity the mind. Sound is in reality the vibratory measure of effort. It in ever-varying circles extendeth its area. If it be uplifting it worketh for good. If of an adverse or mediocre quality, by its disturbing element it accentuates the unrest.

The ability to taste lendeth to the appetite the means with which to appease hunger. The craving for food delineateth the necessity for reinforcing the strength through material means, the physical organism demanding the fuel with which to perpetuate the flame of well-being. Thus the sense of taste, through perverted habit may center on a degrading element. Through the addiction to liquor, to self-indulgence, it may thrust upon soul a pronounced hardship which weakens immeasurably the morale. A perverse habit if indulged promiscuously buildeth a condition which an additional existence must eradicate, the same grade in the school of experience to be undergone a second time, with the initial lesson still unlearned.

When, through self-indulgence, a single sense is blighted soul through cognizance of the predominating weakness must seek within the effect the cause. Perhaps the spiritual vision has been deficient, soul through stubbornness refusing to recognize the Divine Mind, the source of being. Blindness thrusts upon soul the necessity for constructive effort. When the vision is dimmed it automatically deprives of the outlet for activity. It provideth long hours in which mind laboriously and unceasingly probes within the depth of the consciousness, turning to memory for aid in reconstructing the foundation for thought. Blindness is in reality the method through which the spiritual vision becometh an active factor.

When through the failure of hearing the individual findeth the source of sound extracted, soul in increased effort seeketh for that with which to supply mind for activity. It turneth to the panacea the mental development bestows, mind subconsciously being through necessity the organ of renewed activity. When conditions permit, through the visionary ability mind delves within the printed pages, seeking the mental stimulus with which to satisfy its need for companionship. It opens a new field of thought, forcing the soul in question to enlarge its perspective.

When through accident the physical organism endureth the hardship through which a member is severed, it produces a shock of profound proportion. Rebellion, discouragement, anguish both physical and mental—all these tend to awaken soul to the power through which castigation is applied. The hand of love it is which regulates the vicissitudes which soul undergoes, that to it cometh the awareness of the Divine. Perhaps within the past existence soul hath in injury to another builded the condition which, with unfailing precision, the karmic law administers. It may in excessive vanity be made to realize its predominating weakness. Various and innumerable factors enter into the reason for the affliction apportioned. Only the Guiding Force which, with the tender compassion the selfless status bestows, hath the ability to scan the record of past endeavor, seeing within the effect the cause.

The physical organism denoteth the skill of supreme workmanship, its multiple nerve-system, the construction of tissue and bone, the muscular control. To analyze this delicate organism with the scalpel of the surgeon, whose activity is governed by the intellectual ray, is to marvel anew at the Creator's art. The unthinking mind accepteth this, the supreme achievement of physical interpretation, as a natural sequence of Nature. Within the perfected body of the human lieth the cultural instinct and development of eons in which the law of rebirth, with unfailing continuity, has increased the perfective issue, with each additional birth supplying an advance. The incipient ego in its manifestation in physical being is crude in the extreme. Through the intervening periods, in which procreation and gestation are the undeniable factors of progress, soul through affinity functions not as an independent member. The birth of thought following the motivation by instinct lendeth to soul the freedom of individual effort, thence to, with unceasing regularity, alternate in etheric and physical analysis, eventually typifying the development through which the biped known as man emerges.

Oracle Twenty-Two

The divine element which formeth the illumination for soul indicative is of the supreme achievement, it being a fractional unit of the force through which universal control is established. Cosmic the interpretation as is all within the universe. This force of supreme magnitude is in reality the power of the Omnipotent God thus expressed in that which constitutes universal being. No matter what the atom involved, it is sustained through but one power, that which the cosmic essence provides.

The soul, which is of etheric composition (thus we designate for convenience), findeth its sustaining element in the cosmic inflow. The etheric universe, of which the physical is as the shadowy replica, in cosmic interpretation delineates the Supreme Will. Therefore in the hypothesis of being the cosmic force must form the foundation upon which the abstract and relative analysis rests. Flowing from the dome of supreme dimension, this revitalizing, vibrant essence permeates the universal kingdom. It giveth to the vegetable kingdom the procreative instinct through which gestation materializes. It giveth to the mineral kingdom the incentive for the imperceptible transformation through which the refining process is instigated. It produces the element by which the individual soul progresseth from the incipient stage of being into the state where freedom is an assured factor. It provideth the instinct through which the mating of the sexes insures the propagating of the species. Be it of whatsoever denomination, the cosmic element is the force through whose magnitude the Supreme Creator enforceth His omnipotent will.

Relative to the physical universe is to be found the

spiritual antithesis, this being the etheric counterpart. It is the mind which interposeth the veil which separates. Thought being the means by which soul expresses, it, through the concentrative quality, reaches the object of its yearning. Thought, interjected within the confines of space, knoweth no limitation. It, through its resilient quality, rebounds, penetrating the ether and reaching the object of its concentration. The material mind findeth this difficult to accept. For thought, intangible, is as an unexplored area. It existeth. It exemplifies the means through which speech is made feasible. Beyond this the mind in question probeth not, relying on its own initiative to motivate being. Disinterested, it in material aspiration findeth an outlet for activity.

Thought is the urge of Spirit thrusting upon soul the necessity for experience. Through the cosmic interpretation which, vibratory in measure, forces a response in activity, doth Spirit animate soul to expression. The intricate method involved through which is given birth to thought provides a profound enigma to the material mind. Soul, being the spiritual attribute, the motivating agent of the physical organism, the interpretation must of necessity center on the spiritual analysis. To attempt to analyze thought from the physical standpoint is akin to the attempt to leash the lightning, which in the magnitude of supreme power further delineates the cosmic manifestation.

Mind, which is the agent of the soul, lending itself to the manipulation thereof, through the process of thought lendeth itself to the spiritual interpretation. It in reality is the sieve through which soul poureth its content, registered with unfailing precision within the consciousness, which delineates soul's store-house of knowledge. Mind, facile, adaptable, lendeth itself to the manipulation imposed, thrusting upon the brain the necessity for compliance. Co-operative the process involved, mind through the impulse of thought delineating desire.

Desire is the impulse which denotes the innate yearning of the soul. It may in adolescence center on the mediocre, the perverse. It may through inconsequential expression reflect the immature. Through criminal instinct it may denote the retrogressive trend, the astral influence. Or, in constructive effort it may reflect the Guiding Force to which it is receptive. Whatever the quality of thought, it through mind forceth the physical organism to respond in speech or act. To, through control, regulate its quality, demanding obedience of mind, cleansing through pure intent the thought-stream, this automatically lifteth soul to a correspondingly higher plane of consciousness. Innumerable the planes of consciousness which outline the ascent to be made from adolescence to maturity.

The foundation of mind lendeth support to the theory of discarnate being, mind being the outer garment of the consciousness, forming its intricate and perplexing system of control. Mind, being of etheric substance, lendeth itself not to physical analysis. It is in reality the buffer interposed between soul and the consciousness in which it deposits its content. Thought, given birth through soul's insistence, impelled through Spirit's urge, animates mind. Vibratory the process, as is all that existeth in spiritual analysis. It forceth mind to activity, communicating to brain, which is in control of the multiple nerve-centers, its desire. But another process is involved. It leaveth within the consciousness its indelible imprint, there to remain until through the opportunity transition (commonly called death) provides, it is sifted through the sieve of a comprehensive self-analysis, its waste discarded and its treasure retained.

Mind, except when it through mental stress denoteth a profound unrest, reacts to the impulse of thought methodically, registering its content within the receptacle which is in reality the consciousness. It respondeth with alacrity to control. When the fret, the turmoil, of the physical universe produce the disturbance which denotes a mental aberration soul is withdrawn, that, on the healing plane of thought, it respond to the vibratory measure of control. Of healing propensity, it tranquilizes, instilling a deeper sense of peace, strengthening immeasurably this, the spiritual agent. Mind, deprived of its dominating force, is as a weather-vane spinning helplessly on the pivot of subconscious desire. It, from the consciousness, its store-house of thought, grasps at random the memory of past experience in the present or preceding existences, weaving the substance into wierd and grotesque forms, which assume the semblance of reality, tormenting. This accounts for the real or fancied phantoms which confuse the one seeking to alleviate.

Insanity is in reality the condition in which mind, operative through the cosmic inter-penetration, thrusts upon brain the dregs of experience; soul, its motivating and controlling agent, being through divine ordination separated that it undergo a rehabilitative process. Restraint provideth the only means of alleviation.

The consciousness, which accepts the content which mind disburseth through soul's insistence, is as a parchment of immeasurable breadth. It receiveth all, the pure, the impure, the mediocre, the sublime, the degenerative and the constructive, each thought being tabulated according to its intrinsic value; being weighed on the scales of pure intent. The Guiding Force which, unrelenting, giveth supervision to the individual soul maketh possible the experience necessary for fruition. The impulse is instilled through the concentrative process, mind grasping with avidity the suggestion or refuting according to its innate strength. Thought then is given birth in a diversified process, finding its source in soul's insistence, promulgated by Spirit's urge; or through the direct bestowal from the source of interpretative being. The inspirational quality denoteth the pure essence spirituality provides, that soul be immeasurably enriched. The adverse quality through astral proclivity giveth to soul a perverse desire. To deny the power of thought as demonstrated in carnate and discarnate being is to refute the will of the Supreme Intelligence, who thus giveth to all existent souls the ability for expression.

Through control is established the process of thought elevation, habit being the predominating factor involved. When an unworthy or perverse thought through mind's insistence findeth birth, analyze its quality. It must of necessity be uplifting or the reverse if it delineate that which necessitates response. It must be of constructive or destructive import. If it be adverse castigate mind, demanding obedience to but the pure inflow which elevates. Mind may be trained through castigation, becoming not the disobedient but the obedient servant. Thought, reflecting the urge of desire, alone produceth the wherewithal for speech or act.

Oracle Twenty-Three

Equality denoteth the state in which all are as equal, in a like condition. It in reality is the ultimate of each and every soul, the final achievement when soul through the traversing of the karmic cycle hath attained the immortal status. In its incipiency the ego represents a unit of the vast generation which through evolution must function as a separate and distinct intelligence. Spirit must, through the absorption-process, the hibernative issue which the mass-consciousness provides, become the nucleus of the individual soul, thus to, through the path of diversified experience, traverse the cycle to its ultimate completement. A generation of souls issue simultaneously from the dominion, the protective issue, which the mass-consciousness affords, each one through the addition of the companionate affinity to lend support to experience. No two souls traverse the identical path, variety lending the comparative issue necessary to progress.

The socialistic tendency provideth a problem of profound significance. Fostered by the selfish instinct, the supporters thereof desire a disbursement of wealth, each participant to share equally in distribution. The evolutionary cycle, which through its multiple and diversified course provideth soul with the requisites for effort, taketh not into consideration this phase of civilization. Within a generation or a race is to be found the inequality of soul which embraces the adolescent, the mediocre and the advanced. Here are the primary factors of disturbing importance. Wealth may be levelled. But how distribute in equal proportion the treasure of the mind? The profound thinker realizes the necessity for the diversified conditions existent in the soul, the mind, the material exemplification which alone lendeth support to thought.

Universality is the means through which soul denoteth the advanced stage of consciousness. It hath through evolution come into an understanding of the Divine Will. It knoweth whence cometh the strength which motivates, the all-pervading peace through which the fret of the physical universe fadeth away, dimmed to the echo of its former unrest. It, through the compassion which formeth the foundation of thought, embraces all who err; glimpsing, amid the debris of waste the soul disburseth, the divine element which in the ultimate will illumine soul, giving to it the comprehension of the Divine Will. Universality in reality exemplifies the union of soul with the Divine Mind, whose Light it reflecteth in speech and act.

The causation of distress, be it of whatsoever denomination, revealeth an error in thought. Thought, the method through which soul expresseth, trends the path desire indicates as necessary for the gratification of the senses. Thought is the prompter of mind, thrusting upon it the dictum of obedience. If it be of an adverse character, that which disrupts the tranquillity which is essential to a state of well-being, it worketh a hardship. For the brain, responsive to mind's insistence, obeyeth the urge of desire, giving compliance. Whatsoever the result in physical or mental distress, the origin of the experience involved findeth its source in the thought which prompted mind to activity. Therefore thought revealeth the source of all error. To discipline this, the soul's agent, is to control its activities.

Sorrow, which tears to shreds the fabric of life, giveth to soul its true valuation. It, through loss, taketh inven-

tory of the value of pecuniary advantage. It may through
bulk, through surplus, have accumulated a vast supply,
far exceeding that which its individual need demonstrates as necessary for maintenance. Sorrow, thrusting
the blade of anguish within the heart, maketh all else
as naught. Sorrow denoteth the means through which
soul is cauterized. Physical infirmity proveth a near-
kin of sorrow, giving to soul that through which it is
deprived of the partial ability of expression. It may for
a brief period temper soul's activities or through the
course of an entire existence it may teach soul the lesson
of humility, of the subservience of the individual will to
the Divine. It beareth the stamp of divine comprehension, of the inherent and predominating weakness of the
soul involved.

Fulfilment denoteth the completion of the task involved. It bringeth to soul the satisfaction of achievement. Soul, through the objective attained, experiences
a cessation of effort. Thus the orthodox mind vieweth
transition: the physical existence terminated, that soul
soar aloft to its eternal reward. Soul knoweth not completion in the sense implied. As it enlargeth its perspective it embraces a wider field of activity. Service supplieth the incentive through which its scope is enlarged.
It, through diversified means, embraces the universal
conception of being. It, through a unity with the Divine
Mind, drinketh from the fount of understanding, which
gives an increasing thirst for accomplishment. This is
at variance with the existent belief which clings with
unbelievable tenacity to the doctrine of the single existence, refuting in its entirety the law of rebirth. The
Nirvana of suspended effort applieth but to the mind
whose biased belief accepteth not the spiritual interpretation of fact.

Nirvana is the state in which soul through suspended activity liveth in a condition of perpetual bliss. It accepteth the dictum of the Divine Will, which demands naught of effort but giveth to soul a sweet repose. It basketh in the sun of perpetual peace, this to be the ultimate of individual effort. This delineates the haven to which the indolent aspireth. He who through the compassionate instinct visions humanity, glimpsing through the opaque veil of superstition, of greed, of ignorance, its weakness, yearneth not for a state of tranquil repose which heareth not the silent plea of Spirit for assistance but, rather, listens to the voiceless call, torn with the yearning to alleviate, to heal, to illumine the path to the source of the Divine, that, at the feet of the Master, soul cast its burden of woe. Nirvana is in reality the mirror in which the selfish soul glimpseth the image of its predominating desire.

When on humanity Jesus the Master bestowed the priceless gems of His teaching, He gave that which delineated the universal principle. He taught through His healing power the unity of soul with the Supreme Being, whence is derived all that existeth. Through that unity which His faith sustained was lifted the burden of physical infirmity, of mental distress. This was the fundamental principle involved: a faith so profound, so depthless, that it automatically united soul with the Supreme Force which demonstrated a power whose magnitude is immeasurable. Thus was the contact established. Sustaining this was the love which motivated being, the all-encompassing compassion born of the selfless instinct which, through the understanding manifest, probed the depth of the individual need. These priceless attributes were bestowed on humanity as a gleaming example on which to pattern, to mold, the individual soul. Suspended in the annals of historic and literary achievement the outstanding jewel is the Cross, whose radiant significance is undimmed. The unthinking mind reflecteth on this, the crucifixion, as an historical legend whose pathos is profound. Its significance is far deeper. It revealeth the exact process which the individual soul must undergo. It must on the Cross of comprehension crucify its selfish desire. It must through this, the supreme example, come into an understanding of the purpose of being. Only through the acceptance of the crucifixion in its entirety, glimpsing not the ancient significance, but the necessity for the application of the lesson taught, to the present, will humanity find a surcease for its burden of woe.

Oracle Twenty-Four

The cell it is through which propagation is furthered. This provides the receptacle for the ovum through which the complex and intricate system that governs birth is perpetuated. Deposited within the cell, it, through the inter-penetration of the cosmic inflow, bringeth to fruition the incipient ego, the various kingdoms delineating this identical process in varying conditions, regulated by the exact length of time necessary. The seed deposited within the soil, through gestation demonstrates the law of propagative instinct. The embryo is that which is the incipient ego destined in time to become the matured product. Most marvelous and intricate is the process through which the human bringeth into active being the babe. The sex urge providing the mating instinct, the tiny germ through the process Nature provides bringeth into being the facsimile of the adult in miniature proportion, to, when maturity is accomplished, become the individual manifestation. To, in comprehensive analysis, meditate on this, the supreme accomplishment through which the law of rebirth is administered, is to better comprehend the skill embodied. A multiple process is involved through which the canine reproduces, the offspring in a brief period maturing into an identical replica of the parent-root. Nature is the guise through which all life becometh apparent, this being the operative will of the Supreme Intelligence, God.

Gestation is the means through which reproduction taketh place. It is the principle by which is delineated the propagative instinct. It, through the cosmic essence, produceth the replica of whatsoever the object involved: the bee, the flower, the plant. The vegetable kingdom produceth through the process of cross-pollenization, the communion of the infinitesimal organisms through which pollenization becometh effective. The dandelion, with its multiple petals, is the prolific member which is propagated throughout the adjoining territory. To, through microscopic means, study the various methods of pollenization is to emerge in a profound humility of soul, giving homage at the shrine through which is perpetuated the universal kingdom.

The cellular construction through which propagation is fostered denotes the means by which absorption taketh place, the all-embracing wall giving to the incipient germ the necessary support. Ovular in form, it is in reality the replica of the divine pattern which perpetuates being. Within the mass-consciousness is to be found the initial pattern from which Nature copies her predominating characteristic, this being the means through which control is administered to the various kingdoms. The mass-consciousness provideth the wherewithal through which the soul-structure is improvised, it receiving the divine spark, in reality the incipient ego, to, through the intricate process of gestation, give to it the necessary accoutrement for activity. The mass-consciousness, through which control is administered to the various kingdoms, denoteth the supervision of the divine principle. Here is to be found that which through divine ordination is formed through the concentrative effort of the massed souls who, in selfless being, function within the celestial heights. Motivated through the manipulation of the cosmic force, this, the all-protective issue, is evolved. Beneath it function the various kingdoms, each denoting an advance in consciousness, in awareness of the motivating power, this awareness being demonstrated through response. Progressing through the varying kingdoms, mineral, vegetable, animal, we find this, the universal consciousness applicable as the receptacle for the incoming generation of souls which, in incipient form, must of necessity be harbored therein. The mind, through which the soul in physical being functions, understandeth not the intricate process of the inorganic manifestation. It, through the limitation imposed, is restricted in comprehension thereof. The vast realm where, in spiritual antithesis creation is fostered, is the divine conception exemplified. For the Supreme Will ordaineth that the system employed be that which bringeth to fruition the mighty plan as yet unrevealed.

Procreation is the producing of the incipient seed or embryo through which reproduction taketh place. It is the process through which rebirth becomes an active factor. It bringeth into being the individual object, be it of spiritual or physical antithesis. It is the cosmic law of enforcement which through its vibrant essence inter-penetrates the organs involved, bringing to fruition the multiple process of reproduction. The soul, which through descent into physical being is given a new field for additional experience, must through an extensive process of preparation fit itself for that which lieth in advance. It must in a comprehension of its inherent, its predominating weakness, build the morale to the necessary strength to withstand defeat, this being demonstrated beneath the control of the Guiding Force, which control exemplifies the Divine Will.

Cosmogony produceth the means for extensive research. It enlargeth the field for exploration, giving to mind the capacity for concentrative effort. It revealeth the origin of life according to pre-conceived standards. The origin of species as delineated in the current text-books lendeth itself to correction. Far-reaching the perspective if based on the spiritual interpretation of being; but limited if the mind thus occupied restricts its content to that which the physical analysis reveals. The cosmic universe must be the foundation for analysis, the cosmic interpretation alone supporting the building of the system for a true hypothesis of being. Cosmic the power which giveth being, sustaining the universe, both spiritual and physical, in the infinitude of space.

The *cosmic conception,* we may term the creation of the universe. This, the supreme force, generated through the will of the Omnipotent God, lendeth the means through which creation is fostered. It provideth the divine element, be it of whatsoever nature. For all that exists in physical form first finds its creation in the initial spiritual analysis. Thought, which is the means through which soul expresseth desire, must through the cosmic impulse be propagated. The incipient ego must through the separative issue from the Great Whole become apparent, forming the nucleus of the incipient soul. Cosmic the interpretation of universal being, created through the operative will of the Supreme Intelligence, God.

Oracle Twenty-Five

Cauterization is the means through which soul disburseth its accumulation of waste. It is in reality the healing essence of love. A wound, be it of whatsoever character, must of necessity be cleansed, be drained of its adverse content before the healing process is achieved. Thus the Master-Physician, with infinite skill and tenderness ordaineth that the individual soul when necessity demands be subjected to that which produces a reversal of thought. The wheel of plenty turneth merrily to the accompaniment of the hymn of material desire. But when through impediment its speed is diminished, it must of necessity pause to disburse the conflicting element. Desire, through the impulse of adverse thought, maketh the chariot wheels respond with alacrity until, through the weight accumulated, the momentum is slowed to the normalcy growth demands.

Affliction worketh a hardship on the morale. It thrusts the dagger of defeated purpose within the mind, causing a serious disruption of habit. Its means are manifold. It may through physical pain teach soul the necessity for a closer unity with the Divine Mind, which represents the sole source of alleviation. Be it through whatsoever agency relief is bestowed, it cometh but from one source, the Master-Physician. Affliction may through adverse pecuniary condition teach soul the lesson of valuation. The line of caste thus is levelled, soul through understanding visioning all as equal, the divine spark which indicates brotherhood becoming manifest to the spiritual vision. A cleavage from the restricting creed within whose boundaries soul functions may take place, bestowing an additional freedom. Whatsoever the affliction, it teacheth soul the source of its strength.

Physical infirmity is the means through which action is restricted, the slowing of the tempo of physical endeavor. Thus is mind given a stimulus for effort, being through its own initiative forced to motivate. It, through the deficiency the affliction bestows, is compelled to become acquiescent to circumstance. Rebellion, despair, are the emotional outlets through which soul disburses its burden of woe, with, when resignation becometh apparent, a compensating peace.

Anger thrusteth upon soul an adverse condition. It denotes a lack of self-control, a weakness of the morale. Thus emotion is the foe of progress. For, through blurred vision doth soul operate. Numerous crimes are the direct culmination of this, the heat of rage, the murderous instinct becoming apparent. Herein must the astral influence be considered, like to like being the law of progress. The soul in a turmoil of rebellion draweth to it through magnetic affiliation a soul of like status. Thus is additional strength given to effort. Soul on demise taketh with it but that which it hath builded of achievement, be it of spiritual strength or of an adverse character. In astral proclivity function the discarnate exemplifications of lust, hatred, greed; the law of rebirth regulating with unfailing precision the exact plane of consciousness whereon soul functions in etheric analysis, awaiting the descent into matter for additional experience. The dying ember denoteth a decadent condition. Thus must the flame of hatred disintegrate, extinguished through its own fire, that a rebirth of thought take place, giving to soul the impetus for pure intent.

Joy giveth to soul a state of tranquillity. It is in reality the peace of a sustained unity with the Divine Mind. Soul, casting off the fetters the physical plane bestows, centereth its yearning on the spiritual endeavor, which fosters growth. Joy is the ecstasy through which the divine spark illumineth, casting a radiance over thought. Peace is the reflection of tranquillity. It giveth to soul a stabilization through which it becomes a power for good. It knoweth neither rancour nor discord. Soul when functioning on this high plane of consciousness becometh an instrument through which is evolved a masterpiece. It may through the inspirational impetus produce that which enricheth the mass-mind. The healing propensity may in humanitarian effort denote the close unity with the Divine Mind. For thus the true healer worketh, measuring not the content of his gift in material gain. Thus Jesus the Master-Healer gave freely to all who through faith demonstrated their worthiness. Peace is the mirror through which soul reflecteth the Divine.

Ecstasy is the attainment momentarily of the cosmic consciousness. It is the illumination of soul, the radiance of Spirit giving in reality an advance in consciousness. Thus in moments of supreme exaltation the inspired leader incites the mass to response. The evangelist whose spirituality is apparent may, if advanced beyond the stage selfish desire motivates, in self-denial, permeated by compassion, demonstrate the Christic principle; may through leadership set an example of supreme worth. Ecstasy is of necessity of brief duration, soul being unable but momentarily to sustain the high plane which giveth to it the glimpse of Paradise.

Anxiety is the means through which unrest is promulgated, soul through its concern, which mind inflicteth, releasing the emotion of distress. Herein lieth a weakness, will-power being deficient. Soul, if motivated by the faith which sustaineth, accepts the ordeal bestowed, realizing that within all lieth a purpose. Compassionate, the Guiding Force which giveth to soul the element through which it casts aside fear and superstition as an impediment to growth.

Fear denoteth the condition in which faith is a deficient quality. It findeth its birth in superstition, which is a near-kin of defeat. To barricade soul against this intruder, which disrupts peace, close the portals of the mind, demanding obedience to control.

Emotion is the diversified means through which soul disburseth its content of desire. It giveth to soul the experience required that it take cognizance of the varying conditions of defeat as measured against success, of will-power as delineating control and of a deficiency as demonstrating fear, anxiety, sorrow. All these are the combined elements which indicate a weakness of the morale. Soul through compassionate instinct yearneth to alleviate suffering, current distress. It seeks in effort to give what lieth within its means. But the predominating essence of faith motivates the bestowal involved. Through the emotions soul indicates its innate strength. It buildeth or it teareth down. It strengthens or it weakens the morale which alone supports thought.

The varying grades of consciousness may be separated by the control manifest, the means through which mind subservience giveth to soul's dictum. It may in speech, in act, reflect the compassionate instinct, glimpsing the divine element which indicates the spiritual tie that brotherhood delineates. Thus soul knoweth neither rancour nor condemnation. For compassion colors thought. A wide cleft separates the souls in opposite delineation of this rule. One seeth with blinded eyes; one with clear vision. One hath attained the grade of near-selflessness; the other denoteth the selfish purpose which motivates thought. One hath glimpsed the Divine, recognizing the source of its being; the other seeth but the gratification of the senses as the law applicable to present existence. To realize that the transmutation must be made from material to spiritual desire; that compassion must replace condemnation; that the soul who scoffs at the pure, the holy, must through the alchemy of disillusionment, of despair, come into an understanding of its own deficiency—this alone precludes the possibility of adverse criticism. For the soul who condemneth but reflects the weakness still existent within the self.

Oracle Twenty-Six

Through the auspices of power the Supreme Intelligence operateth His omnipotent will. It may be that which bruiseth soul with the futile effort for alleviation. It may be the physical organism through which bodily suffering becometh manifest. It may, in a mental unrest, thrust upon the individual the insomnia of defeated purpose. Soul, being the organ through which the divine element expresseth, thrusts upon mind the necessary condition for growth. It may through the propensity for anguish cauterize the consciousness. Pain is in reality the agent through which the Master-Physician cauterizeth that the healing essence become apparent.

Regret is the remorse through which soul in comprehension striveth to correct error. It is in reality the quickening of the understanding, the process of building anew. Soul taketh cognizance of its error, striving through rehabilitation to correct the fault. Remorse is the means through which comprehension dawns. It is the glimpsing in the mirror of the soul its predominating weakness, the reflection registering with crystal-clearness the extent involved.

Hysteria denoteth the mingled emotions of mirth and pain. Soul trembles on the scales of reason, lacking the initiative for control. A dangerous condition; for of gossamer thinness is the veil which separates soul from the course which mental aberration delineates. Shock, worry, strain—all tend to produce this, the condition wherein the nerve-system in rebellion thrusts upon mind the active delineation of opposite and dual emotions.

Sorrow, with the implication of irreparable loss,

teacheth soul the necessity for retrospection. Through its auspices soul questioneth the mind, demanding proof of continuity of existence. The mind, responsive, lendeth itself to suggestion, probing within the consciousness for a conviction which satisfies. In various means doth soul strive to appease its innate yearning, for Spirit it is which urgeth soul to effort. Sorrow produceth the process through which the hard and brittle shell of selfish desire is punctured, its crystallized surface dissolving beneath the flow of tears, which sear its content. The advanced soul, sustained by its faith, seeth Sorrow as an angel in disguise, a messenger from the Most High bestowing the promise of an eternal spring. The unenlightened soul seeth but a phantom of darkness in the trailing robes of despair.

Grief is the condition which besets soul when the demise of a loved one taketh place. It in its intensity seareth the consciousness, leaving within it the element of despair. Through but one source is alleviation bestowed. The Master-Physician it is who healeth, brushing with tender hands the folds of memory, that they veil from the recipient the sharp outline of Sorrow, the clarity of the draperies by imperceptible degrees assuming a gossamer thinness through which the image reflected is softened to the semblance of a dream. Time, the unthinking mind calleth this, the process of dimming memory; love personified, the advanced soul seeth reflected in the mirror of the Divine.

Soul, the instrument through which the Divine Will operateth, is in reality the cosmic creation. It, through the will of the Supreme Intelligence, becometh adaptable to His purpose. It formeth the active organ by which control is established. It, in unity with other souls of like status, establishes the generation through which evolution is fostered. Detached, it worketh as a separate unit, with the power of individual thought. In unity with other souls, when evolution is complete and soul becomes of immortal status, it respondeth to the Divine Will, which demands obedience. And, operative, it in service demonstrates the law of control. To realize that the Supreme Jehovah, whom man recognizes as God, manifests the power whose magnitude is limitless, that in the superlative heights this Will is through divine ordination made manifest, is to accept the source of power as supreme. Through the mediation of the Beloved Son, the Christic Being, is made manifest this, the law of universal being. Jesus the Son reflecteth the Supreme Will, through the mediatorship of the selfless soul exercising control. Immortality having become accomplished, the ascent through the various planes of consciousness having eradicated all but the yearning for service, for an ever-increasing unity with the Divine Mind—this is the process through which soul selfless becomes, being qualified to, in active exemplification, further the divine plan. Thus serve the invisible Brothers of Humanity who in operative control foster the creative unfoldment of the universe.

The celestial status denoteth the superlative achievement. It is the attainment of the Christic consciousness in which soul hath selfless become. It knoweth but one will—the Divine. It accepteth but the laws which the Christic Being bestows as those through which the universe is subject to control. It functions beneath the understanding which precludes intolerant judgment. Based on love, it reflecteth the divine compassion which is depthless, immeasurable. It, through the affiliation with the Christ, serveth in whatsoever capacity is demanded. No soul chooses its field of service. It liveth within the Law which, irrevocable, apportions that which is unquestioningly accepted. Thus is service exemplified: through obedience, subservience and resignation.

The material mind demandeth proof of the existence of a Supreme Deity. It seeth not within Nature the handiwork of the Divine. It accepteth as happenstance the universe which embraces the physical manifestation, refuting the existence of that which the physical vision seeth not. To attempt to force the conviction of the continuity of life on a plane of spiritual interpretation upon one in this stage of evolution is an exhausting process, the soul in question being not receptive but in a minor degree to Spirit's urge. The babe in spiritual understanding accepteth but the crumbs of the loaf which satisfies the advanced soul. When the adolescent refuseth the sustenance of the advanced teaching, leave to the Guiding Force the unfoldment necessary. Bruise not thine own soul in futile effort for enlightenment. Each soul unfoldeth in accord with a preconceived plan, which knoweth naught of deviation. To force the bud weakens the plant, detracting from its vital energy. Thus must soul, through natural, not artificial means, open its petals to the light of love, which alone provideth understanding.

Religion is the title given to the philosophy which embraces the soul's unfoldment. It formeth the backbone of thought, the foundation of controversial belief. For each stage of evolution interprets this, the divine content, according to its understanding. Therefore countless creeds have sprung up throughout the realm of diversified thought. To rob an individual of the belief which satisfieth the soul is a grievous wrong. For each soul absorbs but the content its craving delineates. Therefore respect the belief of thy associate, taking not the staff which provideth support. Soul when ripe for additional experience, for further exploration in the field of religious interpretation, accepteth naturally the widening horizon of unfoldment, entering therein through the urge of Spirit, which motivates.

Universality is the blending of all existent creeds and philosophies within the mighty cauldron of understanding. Prejudice, antagonism, racial discord—all are dissolved through the divine essence of love, which purifieth and clarifieth the mind, making it receptive to the teaching of the Master who, through the universal principle, demandeth the tie of brotherhood be exemplified, this being the ultimate of the individual soul. Brotherhood is the kinship of soul, the connecting link being the element of Spirit, which is the cosmic interpretation of love. Love is the Supreme Will operative that through its purity, its self-sacrifice, the individual soul reflect its content. Soul, animated by Spirit, when evolution is completed becometh merged within the Divine Mind, functioning as an active part thereof. Love, all-embracing, all-forgiving, giveth all and denieth none.

Oracle Twenty-Seven

The atom which comprises the integral unit of the universe lendeth itself to minute dissection through the microscopic means. It of necessity provides a problem of vast interest. For through unity it becometh the massed content of whatsoever object is involved. The atom lendeth itself to minute analysis. But within its substance must the etheric compound be recognized. For through this, the inter-penetrating essence, is given to matter the ability through which amalgamation taketh place. The atom, permeated by the etheric compound, is impregnated with the cosmic inflow, which lendeth the vital essence. Therefore we must of necessity base our hypothesis of the universe upon the atom, which is the separate unit, the integral part. To further dissect this minute particle lendeth not additional enlightenment. For the term as employed relative is to proportion as delineated in bulk, in massed content. Flowing from the realm of supreme dimension is the force of magnitude through which universal control is established. It is the omnipotent will of the Supreme God, in cosmic delineation permeating space. The spiritual universe, of which the physical is the antithesis, lendeth itself to support through the cosmic power. All creation is thus sustained. The individual soul, which through the evolutionary cycle trendeth its way, the generation of massed souls—all are the active production of the Supreme Will, created through divine ordination to, through cosmic interpretation, delineate His power.

The cosmic force through which the Supreme Will is expressed lendeth itself to a diversity of methods. It, through universal control, demonstrates the supreme power. Directed within the planetary orb, it sustaineth in the infinitude of space. Permeating the individual soul, it giveth to it the means of expression. Animating the infinitesimal grain of sand, it through its vibrant quality maketh possible the unity through which massed content evolves. Demonstrated in the lightning's strength, it in multiple force createth a sense of awe, its magnitude revealing but a fractional part of its intensity. Man accepteth this, the active operation of Nature as a happenstance, realizing not it is the Omnipotent Will expressed. Directed within the channel of practical demonstration, we find light, which maketh of the darkness a negligible quantity. Leashing the current, it demonstrates power. In a diversity of means are the various cosmic agents employed to further the progress of man.

The ageless wisdom embraceth the creation of the universe. The physical universe it is which lendeth itself to this interpretation. For within the supernal heights, the varying planes of spiritual interpretation, creation hath ever been an active factor of the Supreme Will. Functioning in the spiritual analysis, the varying planes of consciousness delineate the evolutionary process. Here function those souls who alternate from physical to spiritual analysis with the precision control affords; who through the operation of the karmic principle demonstrate the law of progress. The physical universe is but the shadowy replica of the spiritual, being but the means through which soul in experience drinketh the dregs of bitter disappointment when through defeat it taketh cognizance of its predominating weakness. To realize that the creative instinct it is which promulgates progress, which affords the incentive for effort, is to turn in reverence to the source from which soul receiveth the impetus for growth.

The spiritual analysis lendeth itself to dissection through but one means. The soul, which through the elimination of selfish purpose hath renounced material desire, which yearneth but to serve in whatsoever field of service is apportioned, through direct communion projects thought within the realm of interpretative delineation; there in humility to receive from the Master Minds the teaching which the Elder Brother hath ordained shall be given to humanity at large, the teaching which shall delineate the universal principle, which shall illumine the path to renunciation, this being the means through which soul selfless becomes, the status which is the ultimate of all. From the celestial heights Jesus, the Christic Being, turneth to humanity, extending the love, the understanding, the divine essence of compassion through which He healed centuries ago. To accept the delineation of the spiritual universe governed through the Christ who in mediatorship representeth the Great Father, to recognize the law of rebirth, not as that which inspireth dread, mingled with fear, but as the eternal spring through which growth is fostered—these truths, accepted, give to soul the assurance through which it looketh through and beyond the veil of material aspiration, glimpsing with crystal-clearness the radiance of the Divine.

Functioning within the supernal heights, beneath the leadership of the Elder Brother, Jesus the Christ, serve the invisible Brothers of Humanity. The supervision imposed is that which selflessness bestows, the predominating desire being that of alleviation. The Christic principle, which is in reality the Law beneath which control is exercised, embraceth the elements of love, understanding, compassion. These are the necessary adjuncts for selfless being. He who serveth in love knoweth not condemnation. He who alleviates serveth thus, prompted by the compassion which, depthless, permeates his being. He who giveth desireth naught of reward; the joy of illumination, of renewed unfoldment, being the compensation bestowed. The Christic principle breathes of universality. It teacheth of brotherhood, the tie which uniteth these, the servants of the Master. This is the ultimate, the supreme achievement to which each soul must aspire.

Jesus the Christ, who as the Elder Brother serveth humanity, hath ordained that certain documentary evidence be bestowed of the continuity of life; that the veil which separates the spiritual and the physical universe be withdrawn; that the soul whose purity is apparent transcribe from the Eternal Records the laws through which shall the dark cloud of spiritual disbelief be lifted from the mass-mind. The revelationary process, this may be termed. The mind which scoffs at the spiritual delineation of being must perforce dwell in the gloom of restricted thought until, through evolution, the soul becometh receptive to the illumination provided. But the soul which seeketh, yearning for substantiation of the laws which govern soul's unfoldment, will find within the current teaching that which satisfies its need. Prejudice and rancour, harsh criticism, must of necessity be the portion of the recording agent. But the illumination which the enlightened soul receiveth in an increased faith and understanding is compensation for the cruel blade of orthodoxy, which is deflected through its own incompetency to give a satisfying interpretation of being.

The *Book of Life,* which certain philosophies designate as the Eternal Records, is in reality the transcript of the Recording Angels. Here lieth recorded the ageless wisdom. For it embraceth the creation of the universe. Beyond this, interpretation is not permitted. The mind functioning through the physical appurtenance lacketh the ability to comprehend. It must of necessity further its efforts on that which the current experience provides. Recorded within this, the divine interpretation, is the record of the individual soul, the laws which further progress, which indicate the control manifest. The creative impulse layeth bare the furthering of propagation, the segregation of souls which in spiritual analysis function in varying stages of consciousness. All lieth revealed. Beyond these, the salient factors of being, lie the laws which govern the progress of the individual soul. These, the Infinite One ordaineth shall be released that he who will may through comprehension thereof lessen the length of the cycle involved; may through control of thought castigate the mind. For in thought alone, which reflects in speech and act, lieth the source of mental and bodily ill.

PART TWO

Oracle Twenty-Eight

Beloved, take thou heed of the words of thy Elder Brother, who speaketh unto thee.

Universal the concept which the mass-mind must embrace. Brotherhood is the means through which unity shall be established. Man must work with and not against his brother.

Unto thee cometh the Living Word, breathing of love, tenderness, compassion. Within the Word lieth the Law. And within the Law lieth obedience.

He who liveth within the Law knoweth not fear. For his soul, *en rapport* with the Divine Mind, casteth out superstition which giveth birth to fear. He who liveth in love reflects the divine radiance. For the Light which eternal is illumineth soul. Draw thou closer to the source of the Divine. For therein lieth thy surcease from pain. There alone lieth the source of thy strength. He who hath not strength, through weakness giveth indulgence to the self. Desire it is which thrusts upon soul the necessity for compliance. He who turneth a deaf ear to desire, which frustrates purpose, knoweth the peace which sustains. In peace alone lieth the tranquillity which gives to soul the power of constructive effort.

Oracle Twenty-Nine

Accept thou the Living Word which shall illumine for thee the path to fulfilment.

Cast from thee the phantom of doubt, which blindeth thy vision to the pure, the holy.

He who walketh in darkness glimpseth not the Light. Within the gloom of the darkened mind all things appear as dark. He who walketh in the Light seeth all things illumined. For the Light within denoteth the Divine.

The mind lendeth itself to control. It inflicteth upon thee the joy of a sustained peace or it heapeth the bitter dregs of defeated purpose. It is in reality the mirror through which soul reflecteth desire.

Brush thou the surface of the mind with the tenderness of understanding, that the reflection mirrored be not blurred and indistinct but with clarity unsurpassed it give forth the image of the Divine.

Within thy consciousness lieth all thou art, the seeds of past endeavor which have through fruition borne the harvest of tears. Unless thou implant the seeds of thy yearning thou canst not harvest the crop of fulfilment.

The empty tare denoteth the blighted grain. Thus worketh the Law. The fruitful harvest exemplifieth the law of fulfilment. According to the seeds implanted within the soil of experience shall be thy harvest.

Man crieth aloud when adversity teareth the soul. Only thus is cognizance taken of the irrevocable law which karma exacts. It giveth or it taketh according to the debt incurred.

Karma delineateth the debt which soul hath con-
tracted, be it of joy or sorrow, of peace or despair. According to the soul's activity doth the Ledger of Life
record the balance.

A debt worketh ill if man payeth not its content. It
hangeth like a monstrous weight upon the consciousness
until lifted through the constructive effort to obviate
its substance.

Oracle Thirty

The Law delineateth the principle of control. It demandeth obedience. He who in subservience maketh submission thereto knoweth not the hardship of adverse condition, for he oweth not that which must of necessity be repaid. He who defieth the Law worketh a profound hardship upon the self. For even as he breaketh the Law, so in turn the Law breaketh the will.

Man giveth of his store of plenty. He withholdeth not that which enricheth his brother. He shareth of his treasure. It depleteth not his content, for manifold unto him is that which he giveth.

Obedience is the submission of the individual will. It defieth not, accepting the Law. He who accepteth not, demanding the operation of the individual will, thrusteth upon soul the hardship of error. As the Law tender is in its irrevocable firmness, so is its harsh discipline manifest if its tenets be defied.

Spiritual the laws which govern the universe. He who accepteth, seeing within each tenet the manifestation of love, knoweth not defeat. For in the acceptance exemplified is obedience to the dictum imposed.

The universal concept demonstrateth the enforcement of the Golden Rule. Man doeth as to him he desireth be done. He woundeth not, for he shrinketh from pain. He stealeth not, for he treasureth his peace. He refuseth not to lift another's burden lest his own prove overheavy. He giveth in love even as he desireth be given unto him. This constituteth the living within the Golden Precept which ageless is.

Oracle Thirty-One

The Living Word floweth forth that within the heart of humanity be given birth the yearning for the Divine. It floweth as a river of peace, which shall within its current sweep away the prejudice of creed. It openeth the portals to understanding, permitting the seeking soul to enter therein. It teacheth of a love that passeth understanding, a compassion which is depthless, a tenderness which is divine. From the source of the Supreme Deity cometh this, the healing essence of love. Through the channel of the Christic Being is delineated this, the Father's will. It receiveth all who will, denying none. It accepteth him who yearneth, embracing with the healing essence of understanding. It cleanseth the heart, instilling the impetus for constructive effort. It giveth the strength which sustaineth in the diversified tasks experience provides.

He who layeth his burden at the feet of the Living Christ receiveth the absolution which repentance bringeth. Repentance demandeth the desire to be born anew. It demandeth the soul rebuild that which it hath destroyed. Soul through comprehension casteth aside the error of adverse thought, delineating the understanding which embraceth the Divine. Only thus doth soul receive the absolution it craveth: by the payment of the debt which through error it hath builded as a barrier to growth.

Oracle Thirty-Two

The vine clingeth to the parent-limb. It sappeth the strength which sustaineth. Thus the weaker soul seeketh support when the storm of life bruiseth. He who supporteth in love knoweth not a dearth of strength. He who casteth away the clinging member shall through weakness find his own strength deficient. Within this worketh a law. He who is weak becometh strong. But it worketh twofold. He who is strong, if pitiless, also becometh weak.

Compassion enfoldeth with love. It bruiseth not. Hatred stingeth with pain, inflicting a wound. Within one lieth fulfilment. Within the other lieth defeat.

Love embraceth with tender arms, lifting the wounded, succoring the weak. It breatheth of the Divine. He who exemplifieth love hath crossed the threshold of enlightenment, glimpsing the source of the Divine.

Hatred findeth its birth in evil. It woundeth with destructive effort. He who woundeth knoweth not love, for he dwelleth in the darkness of a spiritual disbelief.

Spirituality giveth to soul the essence of the Divine. Herein lieth the source of love. Thus the Father giveth, that to each individual soul be exemplified the wealth of His kingdom.

Wealth lieth not in worldly acquisition. It lieth in the treasure of the soul. It amasseth that which eternal is; which fadeth not as the broken flower, but gleameth with the eternal Light.

Diversified the path desire provideth for soul's expression. It leadeth to the pasture of peace. And it lureth to the desert of despair. Soul chooseth the course it pursueth, it through desire expressing its innate yearning.

Desire lureth soul, giving false promise of achievement. Soul turneth to the false, believing therein lieth peace. Peace eludeth until through understanding soul cometh into a comprehension of its predominating weakness.

The Light which illumineth cometh from within. As the candle's flame it flickereth, denoting the inefficiency of instability, until through comprehension of error it burneth with the steady fire of sustained purpose.

He who fanneth the flame of another's soul to adverse effort buildeth that which destroyeth. He who through tender ministration shieldeth until the flickering Light becometh steady buildeth that which is eternal.

Man speaketh glibly of the Light, glimpsing but the material antithesis. Light illumineth. But the eternal Light, which imperishable is, cometh not from without but from within.

Oracle Thirty-Three

The dawn promiseth the fulfilment of the Light. The darkness fadeth as the phantom of the mind. Thus soul cometh into the Light of divine comprehension whence it casteth from it the superstitious belief which is as a barrier to growth.

Soul, through the conflicting emotions, giveth expression to desire. It singeth from joy and it sigheth with despair. Thus it disburseth its content. Each emotion typifieth a stage of growth, giving to soul additional experience.

The Master Intelligence createth the eternal spark. He giveth to each soul alike the divine element. Even as all are created equal in the beginning, so shall the ultimate denote the merging in the Divine, thus establishing the brotherhood through which the Living Christ expresseth His Will.

Through selflessness doth the Christ-consciousness become apparent. The Law demandeth the individual soul upon the cross of its own building crucify the self, thus exemplifying the decree.

Selflessness embraceth the Christic principle. He who exemplifieth this, the superlative status, liveth in the communion of a divine relationship with the Living Christ, serving beneath the tie which brotherhood provideth.

The Christic Being standeth not apart. He receiveth all who seek His living presence. But He cometh not until through the intensified yearning soul lifteth the voice of Spirit, beseeching the Divine Audience.

Communion provideth the means through which soul

entereth the Holy Presence. Within the Silence lieth the spiritual universe. Thus soul in the vast infinitude knoweth neither fear nor distress. For it leaveth the physical means through which it expresseth, entering the haven of the Divine.

The Silence enwrappeth, enfolding the soul which entereth therein with the mantle of peace, this being the means through which the healing essence becometh manifest. Soul emergeth with the armour peace provideth, which deflects the shafts of antagonism, which rebound to their initial source.

Oracle Thirty-Four

The Law worketh twofold. It bestoweth and it sub-tracteth. It giveth the compensation of peace for re-warded effort and it imposeth a pronounced unrest for adverse activity. Soul buildeth or it teareth apart the morale. He who accepteth the Law, dwelling therein, liveth in harmony. He who opposeth, in discord moti-vateth. Irrevocable, the karmic principle regulateth the activity of soul, apportioning that which it hath earned.

The karmic principle representeth the law of cause and effect. As each soul buildeth, so in proportion it receiveth of weal or woe. It knoweth the tranquillity of a deep content or the profound unrest of deflected pur-pose. He who opposeth reapeth a harvest of tears. He who embraceth receiveth the Bread of Life. Thus op-erateth the Supreme Will.

Charity embraceth the spirit of bounty. It giveth; nor asketh in return. In love it bestoweth that which meets the individual need. Charity suffereth long. It supporteth, it lifteth, the weary soul. The hunger which stingeth as a wasp the soul is that which Spirit imposeth. It seeketh to impel soul to effort. It thrusteth upon soul the hunger for the spiritual manna, the thirst for the Wine of Life. He who satisfieth the hungry soul giveth of the alms of spirituality.

When unto thee cometh one in the garments of poverty gaze thou within the eyes, glimpsing the soul's appeal. If humility be manifest, the soul seeketh in love, in resignation. If the stubborn and rebellious soul beseech thee, demanding surcease for bodily hunger, embrace with thy compassion, withholding not the alleviation for bodily ill. He who hungers knoweth not the sustained comfort of well-being, the need manifest denoting the poverty of spiritual understanding or the absence of material means.

Poverty delineateth the means through which soul castigated is. Soul through rebellion hath earned a reversal of circumstance. It must needs turn to the source of the Divine. It refuseth to be led, making necessary the appliance of the lash of adversity. If soul accept the circumstance in resignation, recognizing the working of the Supreme Will, it maketh an advance. If it rebel, long and devious the path ere to it cometh the comprehension of its predominating weakness.

Selfishness giveth to soul a harsh and inharmonious note. It thinketh not of its companion. But it weepeth, it desireth, for the self. It yearneth not to alleviate but for alleviation. It seeketh not to comfort but to be comforted. He who liveth in selfishness seeth in the mirror of his yearning but a gratification of personal desire. He applieth not the Golden Precept. He who seeketh aid must yearn to bestow ere to him cometh the surcease for his pain.

Love, charity, compassion—these are the fundamental elements of the Christic principle. Love embraceth all that exists. It findeth its root in understanding, which embraceth love. Love, all-embracing, all-enfolding, giveth its all, demanding naught. It suffereth, it endureth, it crucifieth the individual self. This exemplifieth love.

Compassion, which is born of understanding, findeth its source in love. Love giveth birth to tenderness, which enfoldeth compassion, tenderness being the outward expression of love. Greater love hath none than he who sacrificeth, who giveth for another his life. This denoteth the supreme sacrifice. He who layeth down his all hath in one act ascended the Cross, accepting the crown of thorns.

Love when transformed by the guise of passion masqueradeth as a foe of peace. It weareth the robe of desire, which giveth not but taketh all. A false friend is he who weareth passion's mask, for passion is but the exemplification of Lust, who buildeth not but destroyeth purity.

Passion weareth a diversity of masks. It maketh entrance in the guise of love. It teareth apart the heart, thrusting within the soul the dagger of pain. It disillusioneth soul, causing it to, in retaliatory measure, robe itself in bitterness. Passion flameth with desire. It seareth the consciousness. If thou wouldst bar from entrance this, the foe of peace, hold before Passion's gaze the emblem of purity, which causeth Passion to grovel in the dust.

Lust findeth birth in evil. It maketh of soul a slave. It thrusteth the dregs of disillusionment, the essence of satiation, upon soul, inflicting a mortal wound. It breatheth of despair. Soul maketh the descent. It consorteth with evil companions; murderous the instinct. He who walketh with Lust knoweth not love. For Lust seeketh but indulgence, which giveth not but taketh all.

Oracle Thirty-Five

Love I give unto thee that thou mayest fulfill the Law.

He who seeketh the treasure which imperishable is asketh not for material gain. He accepteth that which he hath, realizing that whatever be his portion, it is that which he hath earned, that which solaceth his need. It meeteth not his desire, for his desire indicateth not his need. Therefore he who accepteth, murmuring not, walketh in peace.

Peace enwrappeth the soul with the garment of content. It maketh soul immune to hardship, to antagonistic motive. It lifteth, it sustaineth and it healeth. Peace depthless is, knowing neither limitation nor measurement. It cometh from the source of the Divine, being the Father's will expressed. It rewardeth soul for sacrifice, which renunciation is. Peace maketh not entrance within the worldly heart, for material desire barreth the portal. It cometh as the dawn, through its radiance enhancing thought. It leaveth as the twilight, dimming to darkness the soul's expression. It maketh departure when soul through weakness listeneth to Desire. He who walketh enwrapped with peace knoweth neither rancour nor hatred, for in reality he exemplifieth love.

Peace, which maketh of soul a temple whose portals radiate Light, reflecteth the Divine. It knoweth neither partisanship nor creed, for it hath universal become. It draweth not the line of color nor of caste, else how could it reflect love? Therefore, he who maketh a barrier which inflicteth caste, be it of whatsoever nature, barreth peace and weareth but its shadow.

Unto thee cometh the Living Word. It teacheth of the crucifixion of the self. It illumineth the path the individual soul must traverse. It giveth the laws which govern unfoldment. He who accepteth not, refuting the source, denieth the self. He inflicteth upon the soul a denial which impoverishes. Truth cometh from but one source; it findeth its birth in the Divine. It teacheth of the Living Christ, whose compassion embraceth all, whose love enfoldeth, whose tender concern is manifest. The living truth permeateth all creeds, all philosophies. But ever doth it wear the mask which the seeker must penetrate. It lieth not naked. It enwrappeth itself in glamour that the immature be intrigued by its lustre. He who hath made the ascent, whose soul demandeth the naked element, which in renunciation demonstrateth its fitness, its need thereof, findeth in the Living Word the elixir of life.

He who giveth maketh known His living presence through the written word.

Oracle Thirty-Six

The Light eternal is. It permeateth the universe, giving to thought its lustre. It reflecteth the Divine. It illumineth the soul, reflecting the Spirit's radiance. It maketh all things clear to him who seeketh in faith and devotion. The Light which giveth to soul its power of expression cometh but from one source, the Divine.

He who reflecteth the Light reflecteth love. He giveth of his soul's treasure. He illumineth for another the path. Love exemplifieth the Father's will. It omnipotent is. It taketh not but giveth all. If thou reflect the Light thou walkest not in the darkness, which is of the mind. Thus soul imposeth that which bars the Light, making not of mind a servant but in submission giving obedience thereto.

Mind through habit thrusteth upon soul a hardship. It refuseth obedience, through habit giving indulgence to desire. Through control it giveth obedience. A harsh master, it maketh a docile servant when soul exacteth compliance. That which giveth to soul the process of control is the Spirit's flame, which exemplifieth the Light.

Spirit, the divine element, imperishable is, it being the Divine Will expressed. It gleameth as the star when soul submission giveth to the Law. Pure, translucent, it maketh of soul a shrine whose altar eternal is. He who seeth in another the altar of the Divine knoweth not hatred. For his vision embraceth the weakness manifest with compassion, glimpsing in the taper of the Infinite the motivating element.

Soul maketh an altar of desire. It lighteth the taper of peace. The incense of love permeateth afar, revealing the presence of the Divine. He who buildeth thus his temple, permitting his brother to entrance make, shareth of his wealth. He who maketh his shrine, sharing not, dimmeth the taper of his faith, which giveth forth a fitful Light.

Love giveth to soul its radiance. It enhanceth, gleaming in thought as a thread of gold. He who speaketh in love reflecteth the Divine. He who speaketh in rancour delineateth the thread of dross.

The orthodox mind buildeth a temple whose altar barreth entrance to hope. Its taper is as a flame which is dimmed, denying an increased radiance. The taper of the soul should be fanned to an increased brilliancy as each worshipper maketh obeisance at the altar of the Divine.

He who hoardeth his gold, sharing not with the needy, impoverished is. He is as a man who carrieth a cask filled with the nectar of the gods but refuseth to quench his thirst.

The Spirit delineateth the Wine of Life. It supplieth the nectar of being, experience but producing the froth which effervesceth with content or foameth to extinction.

Wisdom lieth within the realm of diversified thought. It embraceth the fundamentals of truth. It exposeth but its surface to the casual passerby. He who seeketh wisdom must seek as for the diamond. Deep within the soil of thought it lieth embedded. That which man extracteth from the surface knowledge is, but wearing the reflection of wisdom.

Oracle Thirty-Seven

Pride denoteth the false garment in which soul enwrappeth the self, flaunting the self-esteem which permeateth thought. As a gossamer veil is this, the web of vanity, for when the harsh wind of adversity bloweth it teareth apart, exposing in its weakness the adolescent soul.

Pride rideth before destruction. It steppeth high, flaunting its tinsel drapery. Adversity plungeth within the heart of pride the blade of poverty and pride seeketh in the dust to express its humility.

Humility denoteth the innate strength of soul. Soul, approaching closer to the shrine of its being, recognizeth the Supreme Power of which it is but the infinitesimal part.

He who in his wisdom speaketh aloud denoteth a false tone. He who in his reticence seeketh in repose to delineate his strength giveth forth the pure note of an advanced intelligence.

Soul accepteth according to the stage of evolution in which it functions. It accepteth the simple broth which denoteth the concentrated substance, or it demandeth the wine through whose effervescent quality is detected not the sustaining element.

He who drinketh to excess imposeth on the mind a supreme hardship. He taketh from its strength that which sustaineth, replacing it with the weakened fibre of a profound regret.

The wine exemplifieth the Spirit's activity. It denoteth the effervescing clearness which giveth proof of life. Or it, through its flat content, refuseth in activity to cast off its inertia.

Evolution giveth to soul the power of expression. Soul dormant lieth until through the tincture of pain it cometh into the awakening of the spiritual dawn.

What matter when the summons cometh on the wings of Time if soul hath in preparedness made ready for the flight? The unfinished task it is which maketh soul to repine, beseeching Time in tones of anguish to delay departure.

Man knoweth not the moment of demise. He calleth the process death, speaking in hushed tones of dread. The transition through which soul ascendeth to a broader field of activity denoteth birth into an understanding which embraceth all that lieth therein.

Caution prompteth soul to speak in idle terms of Eternity, fearing an abrupt entrance therein. The portals of Eternity embrace the universal, each soul in eternal continuity making entrance when through its incipient birth it taketh cognizance of the Light.

Oracle Thirty-Eight

From afar cometh the summons. Soul turneth a deaf ear, refusing to heed. Or it respondeth in a fervor of joy, according to its stage of growth. As a note of celestial beauty or as the sombre tolling of the bell ringeth the call.

Man speaketh of the soul as that which defieth analysis. He speaketh of the mind as a supplement to thought. He seeth not that of which he prattles. But when in spiritual analysis he casteth off the impediment of the flesh he seeth revealed the antithesis of the body as the substance of reality.

The mind is the sieve through which soul poureth the content of thought. Whether it receive freely, without impediment, this, the expression of soul, or whether in its mesh lieth the debris of waste, dependeth on the custodian who in inertia separateth not from the gold the dross.

Mind receiveth the mixed content of thought. It within the consciousness depositeth its substance, there to repose until through comprehension it discardeth that whose waste is as a burden insupportable.

The mind which complementeth the brain maketh not excuse for excess measure. It through compliance giveth obedience. When the toll of experience weigheth overheavy brain in despair rejecteth the content, forcing on mind the backwash of thought. Herein lieth the source of a mental distress which maketh of mind an irresponsible servant.

Service implieth the obedience given to command. He who accepteth in resignation the imposed giveth not rebellion. He who in opposition refuseth to comply buildeth that which necessitates discipline. The Law irrevocable is. It worketh in all fields of activity. None escape its consequence.

The Law worketh for order, which of system is the major part. Intricate this, the espionage which causeth soul to, at regular intervals, reverse its course.

Response is the measure through which soul accepteth the dictum imposed. It refuseth, it hesitateth, and it compliance giveth according to the understanding manifest. He who refuseth learns through pain the necessity for obedience. He who hesitateth, through gentle coercion maketh response. He who obedience gives knoweth the joy of rewarded effort.

According to the response to the summons doth soul denote its spiritual strength. Compensation provideth the means for reward. The peace of a profound content giveth the impetus for joyful effort.

Oracle Thirty-Nine

The *Book of Life* revealeth the source of creation. It hath within its manifold content the wisdom of the ages. Revelation, the thinking mind calleth this, the process of recording therefrom. Communion, the advanced soul knoweth to be the method of interpretation.

The fount of divine comprehension effervesceth with the sparkling waters of truth. Drained of its content, it would reflect the Divine Will made manifest.

The Supreme Intelligence createth the divine element through which soul motivateth. In His supreme wisdom He bestoweth but that through which its sustenance is supplied. Man in his puny strength decrieth the source of his being. But within the mighty reservoir of thought lieth recorded the achievement of the individual soul, there to remain until through fulfilment he scans its utmost content, noting the intricate process of evolution.

The *Book of Life* revealeth the means through which soul attaineth the ultimate. It giveth the laws through which control is made manifest, the laws which form the supervision extended throughout the universal kingdom. Recorded in their pristine beauty are these, the flawless gems of the Divine.

In His own likeness the Supreme Intelligence createth the individual soul. The divine element provideth the urge through which the Supreme Will operateth. Soul, being the complement of divinity, through evolution attaineth the spiritual analysis demanded by the Holy Presence. Soul in its incipiency giveth evidence not of the divine element. It progresseth through the path evolution provides, emerging as a purified substance. Mind, being the intermediary agent, supplying soul with the means for physical expression, becometh a nonentity when immortality denoteth the completed cycle.

The Holy Presence supplieth the individual spark which animateth soul. It is the Supreme Will expressed, that in tangible form it perpetuate experience, the ultimate being the exemplification of the Divine. Soul, through the purification process, becometh the purified substance. It emergeth from the torpor of inactivity, becoming the living, throbbing essence of divinity.

The Holy Presence demandeth the eventual activity of the individual spark. It reposeth, it illumineth and it through evolution returneth to the divine element of its incipiency.

Irrevocable the Law beneath which evolution is fostered. Spirit through affinity demandeth a companionate soul; dual the capacity expressed. Thus motivateth the element involved, that through comparative value soul take cognizance of its predominating weakness.

Mind thrusteth upon soul a hardship, through habit demanding supremacy. To, through control, subjugate mind, denoteth the innate strength through which growth is fostered.

He who maketh resistance to control giveth evidence of a profound weakness. The Law relentless is, forcing to obedience the recalcitrant member.

The Holy See, through which control is enforced, taketh cognizance of the individual soul. Scanning the Eternal Records, the course is changed according to the individual need.

Soul saileth not the uncharted sea. It through divine

ordination pursueth the course designated as applicable to growth, the Guiding Force through innumerable means indicating the course required.

Karma provideth the law of cause and effect, this being the process through which soul disburseth its accumulated waste. Within its tenets no deviation is permitted. Irrevocable its insistence.

Supervision delineateth the means of control. Irrevocable to the soul in physical manifestation these Invisible Forces who control destiny, this being but another interpretation of Law.

Cosmic the element which perpetuates thought, forcing upon the mind the means of expression. Cosmic the motivating force which in universal distribution supporteth the infinitude, which is the immeasurable content of Eternity.

Eternity provideth the ultimate of soul's conception. It comprehendeth not its immeasurable content. The Supreme Deity alone, through His majesty, hath the ability thus to probe the depths of His omnipotent power.

Oracle Forty

Beloved, live thou within the commandments which I have placed before thee.

Love thou one another. Love denoteth the sacred tie which bindeth one soul to another. It provideth the means through which soul compassionate becomes. It findeth its birth within the Divine. For within the Father reposeth the essence of love. Love giveth; nor taketh aught. In unselfishness it yearneth to alleviate. It is all-embracing, all-encompassing, depthless. It delineateth the supreme height of selflessness.

Condemn not lest unto thee shall condemnation be given. He who condemneth knoweth not compassion. Within the soul lieth a profound weakness. For love permeateth not thought. Anger, antagonism, formeth the foundation. He who condemneth reveals the weakness existent within his own soul. He seeth not the Divine in his brother; seeth not the weary length of the path which leadeth to understanding. Give thou of the tender essence of pity, which healing is to the afflicted soul.

Take not from another that which belongeth to the self. He who taketh from his brother shall in turn lose that which he valueth. If he taketh his brother's peace his own soul shall experience a profound unrest. If he taketh his worldly treasure his own wealth shall be likewise depleted. If he taketh his good name, that which he prizeth shall be dragged within the mire. Thus the Law worketh. It giveth to each soul that which it giveth to another, be it of joy or of the salt of tears.

Covet not that which is thy neighbor's. He who yearneth for that which belongeth to another committeth in thought the act of theft. The spiritual law weigheth the thought as equivalent to the act of consequence. For the thought it is which giveth birth to the act. He who centereth his yearning on the acquisition of worldly treasure buildeth that which perishable is; which fleeting is as the dawn, when the harsh wind of adversity bloweth. To covet that which is not thine own denoteth the jealous instinct. The soul in question hath not made of the mind a servant; it in desire reacheth out for additional acquisition.

He who lifteth his brother, who giveth the helping hand, who sustaineth in love, buildeth for the self the elements of spirituality. This denoteth the spirit of sacrifice, which withholdeth not that which easeth pain, which alleviates, which lightens the load whose weight is crushing in its intensity. The burden may be of a mental unrest. It may be of a physical nature when the karmic law demandeth a readjustment. It may be that which poverty imposeth, bringing to the object the hunger, the privation, of want. Whatever the nature, he who giveth in love receiveth in proportion to that which he giveth.

Seek not to take from another that which satisfieth his spiritual yearning. If the creed in which soul is immersed bestoweth the manna which alleviates the current need soul must perforce continue absorbing that which it craveth, until through growth the mental hunger is extended beyond, embracing a wider perspective of thought. Worship lieth in the homage, the adoration, of the soul presented at the shrine of its spiritual understanding. Naught barreth the supplicant who seeketh in humility the source of its being.

Seek not in retaliatory measure to wound thy brother. If the shafts of antagonism, of hatred, are directed against the citadel of thy faith thou mayest deflect with the healing essence of love. Hatred pierceth not the armour of love. He who giveth in return of adverse measure knoweth not the joy of fulfilment. For the soul denoteth the absence of understanding. To glimpse not the dross which represents the weakness, but rather the pure gold which is the Spirit's flame, is to disarm hatred with love.

He who walketh with love walketh in peace. The green pastures delineate the plane on which the soul functions when desire, when yearning, is centered on the spiritual attainment. It seeth in the physical existence a grade through which soul must pass to learn an invaluable lesson. The Valley of the Shadow exemplifieth the darkness of spiritual disbelief, the light of love permeating not its depth, illumining soul, which thus glimpseth the Divine.

When thou walkest with fear by thy side thou art oppressed by superstition. Thou seest the phantoms of the mind which are as the shadows of the darkness. Disburse thy mind of fear. For fear it is which thrusts upon soul the profound unrest through which it heareth not the soothing voice of reason. The Valley of the Shadow seemeth not dark to the soul whose faith illumines its length. It seemeth as but a step across the threshold of the Divine.

Cast not the cold stone of censure at thy erring brother. He but walketh the path which thine own feet have trod. If thou through comprehension hath lifted thy soul to a higher plane of consciousness, even so must thou advance again, following in the footsteps of thy brother who precedeth thee. Thou must look before thee, that thy vision become not obscured. Thy brother looketh to thee for example even as thou lookest on high for the ideal on which to pattern.

He who sinneth must first in thought commit adultery. The thought giveth birth to the act. The law demandeth the witness give evidence as proof. The spiritual law ordaineth that the soul which in thought is guilty of sin pass before the bar of unprejudiced and unbiased judgment, the Spirit thrusting upon soul a cognizance of its own error.

The Magdalene symbolic is of the lapse of virtue, this being but another delineation of Nature's delinquency. The propagating instinct thrusteth upon soul desire. The weakened morale demonstrateth not the strength resistance provides. He who hath made of mind an obedient servant knoweth not the lust of desire. For mind, obedient, denieth entrance to the impure, the unclean. The Magdalene constitutes that which thinketh ill, which lusteth in thought. Thus the spiritual law defineth adultery.

The universal concept teacheth that each soul in worship findeth its strength. Through communion soul seeketh the source of the Divine, lending itself to the healing inflow of love. It seeketh when the need becometh manifest. It denieth not the craving for communion. It setteth no day apart as one of worship, for it liveth within the law which demands soul seek in an ever-increasing fervor the spiritual manna. It hath passed beyond the restricting barrier of creed. It maketh of each a holy day. This confuses the orthodox mind which, systematic, setteth apart the Sabbath for communion. Creeds afford the support necessary for the soul dependent on the guidance of the pastoral head. Leadership giveth the incentive for renewed effort. But the soul whose horizon embraceth all philosophies and creeds, their intrinsic worth merged into the universal concept, seeks in solitary worship, in meditation, the unity with the Divine Mind which giveth the tranquil calm of a supreme content.

Oracle Forty-One

Creed supplieth the means through which soul out-lines the path its innate desire indicates as meeting its immediate need. It accepteth the nourishment offered as that which satisfieth. It permitteth the tendrils of the mind to extend when the soul functioning therein needeth a wider field of thought. Herein lieth the weakness. That which restricts lendeth a hardship. The soul, the mind, through a constantly increasing expansion giveth evidence of growth. Thus experience provideth the means of diversified exploration. Soul, when the current belief ceases to satisfy, when the spiritual brew seemeth stale and flat, should with the ease of a precon-ceived understanding gravitate toward a more liberal exemplification of spiritual enlightenment. It denoteth naught of disloyalty. It meaneth that through growth soul desires a richer vintage with which to satisfy its spiritual craving.

Theosophy embraceth a diversity of fields. It giveth to mind an inexhaustible supply in which to explore the various interpretations of being. That which is as meat to one soul satisfieth not its companion. Each soul, ac-cording to its individual need, seeketh the exact phil-osophy which satisfies; diversified the content. The Eastern mind in the occult findeth the outlet for expan-sion, the temperament of the Oriental lending itself to the glamour its significance delineates. The Western mind, more prosaic, less elastic, findeth this, the subtle essence, inadaptable. For the senses, through control, are less facile, less given to long hours of concentration in which the body lendeth itself to harsh and severe discipline. The cleft which separateth these, the varying stages of growth, is that which evolution provides, each accepting the manna the Divine Law apportions. To attempt to force soul into that for which it obviously is unfitted worketh a hardship. The Continental Divide which separates findeth its parallel in the spiritual delineation, each soul through preordination functioning in the exact groove its stage of evolution provideth as necessary for consistent growth.

Race provideth a dilemma to the immature mind. It seeth not the Divine spark which animateth. It seeth but the varying color-tones of the skin pigment. That which separates one race from another is not the outward semblance of difference. It is that which evolution provideth. To realize that soul on its migratory journey taketh the individual characteristics from the race in which it for the time being functions is to better understand the reason for the variance in habit and belief. Evolution alone apportioneth to each soul its exact plane of activity. Thus are the varying religious beliefs exemplified, each race through inherent tendency responding to the teaching which has been provided for its existent faith. The intricate wisdom of the Supreme Intelligence giveth to the individual soul, on whatsoever plane of consciousness it functions, that which provides incentive for growth.

Oracle Forty-Two

The written Word compriseth the Law, which irre-vocable is. Man deemeth the Law that which subject is to alteration. But within its tenets lieth the Supreme Will made manifest. The Law demandeth the subservi-ence of the individual soul. It worketh for the ultimate good. The divine spark, which in incipiency illumineth soul, must needs be fanned into the glowing flame through which is Spirit's strength exemplified. Evolu-tion provideth the course through which each soul must trend, purity being the ultimate. Man sayeth: the indi-vidual through his own volition maketh choice of that which experience provides. The Law replieth: experi-ence, subject to control, giveth that which the individual soul needs. Thus readeth the Law.

Happenstance entereth not within the law of cause and effect. Within all lieth a purpose. Soul taketh cog-nizance of a near-element of danger. It rejoiceth at the escape therefrom. This worketh through a preconceived plan. It teacheth soul through shock the necessity for caution. It giveth a sense of insecurity through which soul seeketh within the consciousness for the reason therefor. The Law irrevocable is. It varies not from its compensative issue. It giveth of joy or sorrow, of care or freedom therefrom, that which soul hath earned.

Law worketh for control. It establisheth supervision. It teacheth obedience. It maketh of the individual a servant, be it in whatsoever manifestation. From but one source is control demonstrated—it is the Supreme Will operative through mediation. It ruleth all that exists, extending throughout the universal kingdom. Knowest thou one who liveth not within a law? The Law embraceth all existent elements, each lending to a subsidiary control. Nature through innumerable guises demonstrates the Supreme Will. It lendeth that through which the physical universe exists. It supplieth all that satisfies, that sustains the creature and the human. Nature is the Supreme Force through which the Omnipotent God worketh His will.

The Supreme Will worketh that to the universe be given the wherewithal for continuity. It supplieth the force whose magnitude, immeasurable, sustaineth creation. Cosmic the delineation, this being the operative Will expressed. Within Eternity lieth that which exists in endless continuity, that which hath neither beginning nor end. Thus the Great Jehovah veileth the source of being. The mystery of creation, man calleth this, the impenetrable. The Immortal, who hath through purification attained the perceptive ability, vieweth the universe in its entirety. The Cosmic Mirror, in reality the mirror of perception, revealeth in its entirety that on which he focusses his concentration. It knoweth naught of impediment. For, having through selflessness returned to Spirit manifest, the dross extracted from soul through the crucifixion of desire, the divine element exerciseth its rightful heritage. It penetrates all existent matter. All lieth revealed. Cosmic the essence of being. It penetrateth all, knowing naught of resistance. The divine spark, through its creation being an infinitesimal fraction of the Great Whole, cosmic is. Enwrapped within the cellular folds of the mass-consciousness, through absorption it formeth the soul-structure. This, the enwrapping garment, through the cycle evolution provides becometh the purified substance, giving to the divine element support, the means for individual expression. Thus formeth the individual soul, being the supreme achievement of the Divine Will.

The heaven-world compriseth innumerable planes of consciousness. Man seeth this as an extent of thought. The Immortal seeth this as a state of being, segregation perpetuating the Law in all grades of progress; like to like being the Law; the ascent being made through the demonstration of the soul's fitness for the advance. Service denoteth the means through which growth becometh apparent. The soul, which in evolution expresses through the auspices the mind affords, thinketh itself a free agent. It seeth not the supervision manifest from the realm of spiritual delineation. It detecteth not the Guiding Force which through suggestion, through concentration, controlleth effort. It glimpseth not the working of the Law, whose precision varies not a hair's breadth from fulfilment. It, through diversified experience, learneth its innate weakness. And it taketh cognizance of the futility of error. Experience teacheth resignation, endurance. It maketh of soul a servant. Soul thinketh itself the master of its destiny. Experience denotes the mastership which breaketh the will, forcing soul to implicit obedience.

The spiritual antithesis of being affordeth soul the opportunity for retrospection. It vieweth as a vast panorama its activity from incipient being to the present status. It seeth the weakened thread in the fabric of the soul and it through comprehension thereof buildeth anew. It returneth to, in an additional existence, test the strength, continuity of rebirth being the law through which purity becometh apparent. Rebirth provides the necessity. For each respondeth to the Law through which Nature propagates the species, be it of whatsoever order. The human denoteth the advanced handiwork of Nature, for thus worketh the Supreme Will. He who giveth to Nature the soul's homage but expresseth the

appreciation of the Divine. The Law apportions to each
object the exact sphere in which it functions as that
applicable to its immediate need. The etheric counterpart obedience giveth in spiritual interpretation, thus
demonstrating the law of growth.

Consciousness embraceth the ability for understanding. It denoteth the innate strength of soul as expressed
in thought. It hath within its element the urge of Spirit,
which through soul motivateth being. It is the means
through which the Supreme Will operateth in individual effort. Consciousness in reality is the individual
expression of the understanding of the Divine.

Consciousness giveth to soul the wherewithal for exploitation. It provideth the receptacle wherein thought
registers its accomplishment. It retaineth all, giving to
soul the privilege of extracting therefrom that through
which it expresseth. It may be a storage-house of power
of a superlative order, that through which it enricheth
humanity. Or it may through its adverse character become a deterrent force. It is the means through which
soul disburseth its predominating desire. He who hath
attained the superlative state demonstrates the Christic
consciousness. To this must each existent soul aspire as
the ultimate achievement.

Consciousness hath a twofold meaning, which confuseth the immature mind. It denoteth a state of achievement and it likewise proveth the store-house of knowledge. When soul through the purification process hath
become the purified substance it discardeth mind. Mind
through the process of absorption becometh as one with
the consciousness, merging its substance therein. When
soul through the spiritual attainment delineates the
supreme achievement it, through purity, reflecteth the

divine impetus. That which it hath through process of concentrative analysis retained as wisdom findeth its source in truth, which is of divine origin. Therefore soul, having attained the Christic consciousness, draweth from its content, which is of like character, the consciousness being the awareness through which soul expresseth the Divine.

Jesus the Christic Being, who through the crucifixion exemplified the supreme example of selflessness, delineateth the mediatorship through which the Omnipotent God expresseth His august will. In universal control is this power vested. Through the advanced souls whose superlative attainment demonstrates their selflessness, their worthiness, doth the Living Christ exemplify the Supreme Will. From the supernal, the celestial, heights is control manifest. Through innumerable channels doth this mediatorship extend, penetrating the heart of humanity.

The cosmic essence, which is the divine force, regulateth the universal pulse, slowing its tempo when necessity demands through the process of castigation superinduced by that love, that understanding, whose depths humanity is powerless to probe. No soul existeth in etheric or physical analysis whose yearning is denied to, from the Living Christ, receive the solacing peace which is His gift of love, of faith, superinduced through the soul's renunciation of selfish purpose, of material desire. Soul within the Silence findeth the source of the healing essence, emerging refreshed, with renewed strength. Whatever the soul's need, it in communion findeth that which uplifts, sustains. To realize that the infinite compassion, the depthless and all-embracing love, which through the supreme sacrifice gave to hu-

manity the ideal of superlative beauty, is but the symbol
of that which in active delineation revealeth the source
of soul's individual effort is to, in comprehension, approach the shrine of individual worship, seeking within
the love exemplified the healing inflow of peace.

Oracle Forty-Three

The Law in the ultimate maketh all as equal. The incipient soul which in group-form issues forth from the enveloping folds of the mass-consciousness knoweth no separation, the generation involved migrating on through the varying and diversified experiences which outline the evolutionary cycle, accepting individually the apportioned path, each adapting to the individual need that which lieth therein. Thus evolution provideth the means for unfoldment. When through the eons necessary for the exemplification of the purification process the soul emergeth as a purified substance, functioning through the profound awareness of the Divine Will, it hath accomplished the ultimate. It through selflessness delineates its fitness, its worthiness to, in unity, serve humanity beneath the direct supervision of the Master Jesus. Thus function the invisible Brothers who delineate the Christic teaching.

The pseudonym, the *White Brotherhood,* lendeth support to various misleading interpretations. The advanced soul whose spiritual understanding accepts the active delineation of a vast group of selfless souls, who in service exemplify the Supreme Will—it unhesitatingly realizeth that control is the sole means through which order is established and maintained. When the spiritual vision is quickened, giving to the soul an awareness of the spiritual counterpart of the physical universe, it glimpseth the aura of these, the Master Servitors. Thus hath the white-robed Brother become an accepted factor in the delineation of spiritual being. The material mind, with the understanding adolescence provideth, derides that which its immaturity prevents it from dissecting. The aura, being the outer garment of soul, the luminous radiance which Spirit reflecteth, provides the apparition of a white-robed Being. United by the dominating desire for service, responding to the love-essence which in ever-increasing intensity permeateth being as soul ascends higher in the scale of consciousness—thus serve these, the selfless Beings who delineate through active supervision universal control.

The Silence provideth the haven for the soul. Within it soul casteth aside the fret of the physical plane, ascending to the realm of peace, this being the height of its innate yearning. When in physical being Jesus the Master descended to create an ideal of superlative and eternal beauty, he when necessity demanded withdrew, that in the Silence of a profound communion He might through the Divine Audience receive that which revitalized, which lifted soul, instilling the peace, the tranquillity, the spiritual strength through which it impervious became to the hardships necessarily imposed. He withdrew, ascending to the Mount of a supreme peace. From this high and superlative plane of consciousness He bestowed upon humanity the essence of His compassion. He spoke in words of wisdom so profound, so sublime, that they are engraven in eternal sequence upon the Sands of Time. From the heights He giveth forth that through which shall humanity cast aside its burden of woe, its fret, its evil proclivity. Thus He speaketh:

Beloved, unto thee cometh the Spirit of the Living Christ; tender, compassionate the love which enfoldeth, which embraceth. From the celestial heights cometh the Voice, which through its yearning shall pierce the heart of humanity. He who yearneth shall drink from the Living Waters, shall quench his thirst. His hunger shall be appeased, for he hath found that which eternal is. He who turneth away, rejecting this, the Bread of Life, knoweth but the despair of defeated hope. The path lieth in advance through which each soul must pursue the phantom of peace. But unless his vision embrace the spiritual he findeth not reality. He who turneth in yearning to the source of the Divine knoweth not want. For soul in faith accepteth the Living Word, dwelling therein. He who seeketh for the bauble of material desire findeth not the pure gold which alone satisfieth. The healing essence floweth forth to him who will. It breathes of peace, of love. It is as a fount in which soul immerseth, through rebirth coming forth anew. The morass of fear, of illusion, in which the soul of the recalcitrant bathes leaveth but the desire of the flesh, which as an insupportable burden teareth apart the morale. He who will may enter the Holy Silence, therein finding the soul's retreat. There is Spirit through the divine essence fanned to the intensity of renewed flame. There is selfish purpose crucified on the cross of renunciation. There is love born from the yearning for service, for the alleviation of the suffering which afflicteth humanity as a monstrous ill.

The Living Christ speaketh unto thee. Through the channel made adaptable through preordination He addresseth humanity, extending compassionate hands, pleading that he who suffers turn to the source of the Divine, to accept the Light which faileth not. What matters worldly desire if it be that which perish as the harsh wind of adversity bloweth? Fragile as the dawn is the material treasure. That which breathes of divinity alone survives, being the imperishable and divine gift of love. Man in selfishness seeketh in indulgence the surcease for his pain. Indulgence is but a depthless morass in which soul striveth to immerse its unrest. Compassion must be the predominating yearning of the soul. It must teach that only he who giveth receiveth in return. Man reapeth but that which he soweth. He gathereth but the harvest of his yearning. He soweth the adverse seed and he reapeth the harvest of regret, of remorse. The gold becometh not the pure metal until it hath renounced through alchemy the dross. The soul findeth not peace until it hath in renunciation cast aside selfish desire. He who cometh in faith, in yearning, findeth the panacea for his pain, his unrest. If he lifteth his soul in supplication the tender embracing love healeth, permeating soul. Thus is the Divine Presence made manifest; soul receiveth the assurance that it seeketh. If he turneth away, refusing the call, he must in unrest seek until soul, worn, weary, once again taketh heed of the summons.

He who speaketh yearns to solace, to heal. In living thought He giveth forth the Word within which lieth the Law. The Living Word goeth forth that to humanity be given the assurance of eternal continuity of the soul; that it illumine the path which soul must trend that the ultimate achievement be accomplished. It offereth the compensating peace which alone healeth. For within it lieth the supreme and sublime assurance of love.

Oracle Forty-Four

Various creeds delineate the religious principle. He
who findeth that which satisfies his need must of necessity absorb the content. The basic principle denoteth
the element of truth. Creed giveth to soul the support
through which, beneath its guiding head, soul unfolds.
According to its innate need, demonstrated by the understanding manifest, doth soul respond. To separate
from the individual the manna which satisfieth is to rob
of its peace the supplicant. Soul unfoldeth as the flower,
the petals of thought responding to the divine impetus.
Mind, through its facile adaptability, delineates an ever-
widening perspective. It, through the inflow of thought,
more deeply entrenches its tendrils within the soil of
diversified interests. When through yearning it reacheth
out beyond the restricting boundary of its present philosophy it exemplifieth the normal law of growth. To
deny the craving for additional enlightenment is to
thrust upon mind an acute hardship. To, through restraint, refuse soul, mind or body the expansion Nature
demands is to thrust upon the member employed a near-
paralysis. Creed in reality formeth the guise in which
soul through absorption satisfies the craving for the
spiritual manna.

Jesus the Master, through His infinite compassion,
His divine tenderness, exemplified the essence of love.
He gave unstintingly, withholding naught which might
enrich humanity. He, through the healing essence, lifted
the burden of physical infirmity. He freed the soul of
the obsessed. He lifted the veil that those who would
might see. All these were the priceless gifts of His beneficence. Through the ideal presented countless souls
have patterned on this their individual efforts. Jesus,

the man, standeth forth as a gleaming light to which the passing centuries have but added a deeper lustre. From what source came this, the Divine Healer? Descent was made from the high status of celestial being through the auspices of physical endeavor that to humanity be given a glimpse of the sublime. He who in reverence turneth to the shrine of the crucifixion knoweth that in the example presented lies far more than a mere allegorical figure. The Supreme Intelligence willed that the beloved Son should through rebirth give to humanity the supreme ideal; that the crucifixion of the body should in reality delineate that through which each soul must pass, with its corresponding anguish. On the Cross of its own building must desire be crucified; must selfish instinct become non-existent. Jesus through example taught the multitude the art of divine healing. The channel must first be cleansed; be made pure and holy for the Divine Fire, which of necessity cometh in response to renunciation. No healer may in turn transmute the illness of the flesh into a state of non-existence unless first he hath through purification become innately pure. Thus readeth the Law of divine interpretation. Jesus the Healer gave lavishly of His wealth of love. He received, He accepted, naught in return. So doth the Law read: that the spiritual, the divine, element be given freely; nor debased through the pecuniary value set on its essence. Jesus through compassion, through a yearning to alleviate, healed those who besought Him in faith. He who approacheth the Shrine of the Divine in faith maketh the self receptive to the divine inflow. He who hath not faith receiveth not. Thus readeth the Law. Faith is the predominating and the necessary attribute of the supplicant who craveth the divine healing. The broken vessel which lendeth itself not in recep-

tivity maketh useless the efforts for repair. He who
enricheth the self through the manipulation of a spiritual endowment contracteth a debt of supreme magnitude. If man accept the ministrations of Jesus as the
supreme pattern no deviation is possible, from their
tenets. Of humble mien, tender, compassionate, the
Savior of men mingled freely with the multitude. Herein lieth a lesson of profound import. Pride, which delineateth a weakness, draweth the line of caste, which is
as a cruel barrier. It separateth as by an impregnable
wall the individuals or the nations concerned. Wherein
lieth pride? All souls created are as equal. All souls
emerge in the ultimate as equal. Of what account is the
material treasure which giveth caste to society? Wealth
denoteth a surplus of plenty. The humanitarian instinct
which shares its excess worketh for good. The instinct
which in lavish waste shareth not its surplus, will in
the final analysis once again enter into physical being
to, from poverty, learn the lesson of equality.

Brotherhood delineateth the unity of souls in which
love is the predominating factor, love which shareth,
which lifteth the burden of woe, be it of whatsoever
nature. Love giveth freely of its all. If a nation or a
people take each from the other in greedy instinct love
entereth not. For he who loveth giveth. Greed is as a
serpent which twineth its coils around the soul, restricting its growth, the only manifestation being in an increased measure, as soul through weakness giveth assent
to the embrace.

Greed is the monstrous sore which hath spread over
the heart of humanity; corrupt its measure. Herein
lieth the cause which produceth the effect; unrest, with
an ever-increasing pain, being the offspring of greed.
Humanity heareth not the call. Immersed in its own

unrest, it turneth from the Spirit's urge, repudiating
its rightful heritage. If a man lose his own soul wherein
lieth the gain? Eternal the treasure of the Spirit. Fleeting the false manifestation of desire.

Selflessness denoteth the Christic attainment. Selfish
desire hath been transmuted into the compassionate
instinct; love, the predominating factor, a love which
breathes of sacrifice, of devotion, that which lifteth,
healeth the bruisèd, the weary. Couldst thou vision a
world devoid of love? Love alone maketh of soul a Light.
It alone provideth the radiance which illumines, which
as a halo enhances thought. Be it in an inspired leader,
a theme of superlative beauty, it findeth in love alone
its gleaming significance. Were love to be extracted
from the cultural delineation of the literary realm,
flat and colorless would be the remaining content. Love
glorifieth the soul which reflects the Holy Radiance.
Love, the supreme, the divine attribute, cometh from
but one source. It is the direct reflection of the Father's
all-embracing tenderness giving to soul its motivating
Light.

Love giveth and withholdeth naught. Within these
words lieth the achievement of the supreme sacrifice.
Jesus it was who through subservience to the Divine
Will ascended the cross, thereby crucifying the self.
Love, the predominating factor, supplied the necessary
strength; the worship, the adoration of the Supreme God,
lending support. He who through selflessness exemplifieth the supreme ideal, from the celestial heights reacheth forth to humanity beseeching the individual soul to,
in like measure, approach the great Shrine of Universal
Being. To the Father must be expressed the soul's homage, its adoration. For therein lieth the source of all.
To the Son, the Mediator, must humanity turn, seeking

therein the healing essence of alleviation. Humbly must the supplicant bow to the Divine Will. Humility is but the spiritual garment with which soul enwrappeth the self. To, in subjection, submerge the individual will but enriches immeasurably the mind. From the measureless reservoir of thought man extracteth but an infinitesimal, a fractional, part. He who realizeth his deficiency hath made a step in advance. For pride is as a portal sealed, which barreth entrance to enlightenment. From the heights of divine comprehension is bestowed this, the Master's message, that to humanity be given the Light which shall illumine for the seeker the path.

Oracle Forty-Five

Religion giveth to humanity the ideal on which to pattern. It affordeth the means through which soul taketh cognizance of the Divine. It is in reality the staff on which humanity leans in moments of distress and anguish. The individual soul interprets religion according to its understanding, thus evidencing the stage of evolution in which it functions. Religion embraceth innumerable and diversified creeds, each one delineating the path its narrow confines afford for the expression of the souls motivating therein. Various philosophies offer conflicting statements of the origin of the soul, each one based on that which its potential head accepts as the true delineation. Confusing in the extreme to the soul who, in an extensive research, seeketh to probe the mystery of being. Religion is the concept which giveth to humanity the awareness of a universal God, a Supreme Being. The true interpretation of this, the definition of God, may be summarized in a brief sentence: religion embraceth the seeking of the Divine and the acceptance of the Word, which is the Law. The subservience of the individual will, the willingness (the obedience which constitutes resignation) to accept the supreme ultimatum—this is the initial step toward a unity with the Divine Mind.

Religion delineateth the means through which soul unfolds. It giveth the foundation to thought. Be it of the mediocre or the intellectual, within its content lieth the basic foundation of religion. This statement the thinking mind may refute. The criminal denoteth the soul devoid of religious principle. Hardened, calloused, of evil propensity, it lendeth itself not to the guidance, whatsoever the source, which attempts to, in compassionate effort, instill a yearning for enlightenment. The adolescent, thoughtless, irresponsible, through the irrelevancy of superficial attainment seeketh the froth of life with which to satisfy desire. Should calamity thrust upon the soul thus delineated the dregs of sorrow, childlike it turneth to the source of the Divine, instinct guiding the impressionistic nature. The more advanced soul, brittle, ofttimes rebellious, through an innate and instinctive antagonism refuseth the suggestion of the spiritual analysis, relying on its own strength, its own initiative, for effort. Here lieth the impregnable element. For, materialistic, it placeth upon the worldly attribute the value of a false conception. Bitter the experience which teacheth such a soul its innate weakness. To, in compassionate regard, understand the varying stages of soul-growth, lending through example the pattern which through its beauty inspireth admiration—this is the means through which response is induced. The barren soil receiveth and nourisheth not the fertile seed. Cast within the precincts of a religious disbelief, it will but perish. Therefore refrain from bruising thy soul by entering the prejudicial confines of an antagonistic mind. Leave to experience, superimposed by the Guiding Force, the means through which capitulation taketh place.

Religion embraceth various philosophies which through their separation denote a wide cleft of thought. Study, with the understanding enlightenment provides, the massed souls embracing the faith in question. Here we find functioning a group of souls whose evolution denoteth a similarity. It may be the need of guidance, as delineated by the supervising head, is the only means through which effort is fostered. Perhaps the unity lendeth strength. It may be that the kinship which is instinctively, subconsciously acknowledged, uniteth this group to, in additional experience, further growth. Various reasons there are for such an association. To separate the threads which unite these philosophies is as to tear asunder the biblical interpretation. The fundamental principle is based on truth. It may be the gossamer veil of illusion, of glamour, of mystery, enfolds; intriguing the seeker by its apparently impenetrable depths. According to the individual soul doth the interpretation intrigue, the innate need demanding that which it represents.

Evolution embraceth all grades of matter. It, through growth, through unfoldment, denotes the presence of the divine element which motivateth. The mineral kingdom denoteth a constantly changing metamorphosis, each element therein vibrating with the cosmic essence of being. The floral member, which through the vegetable kingdom delineateth Nature's versatility, giveth evidence of an increasing breadth and scope. It, through the rebirth spring affords, in perennial beauty radiates the divine interpretation. The animal kingdom, from the lower forms of dormant analysis to the intelligence the canine affords, giveth evidence of a superior creation. The human, which alone motivates through the divine attribute of the soul, reflects the divine urge, the constantly increasing expansion of the mind. The infant through its insufficiency hath not the power of expression in speech. Through the auspices of Time it casteth away the immaturity of childhood, in adolescence denoting growth. Maturity giveth the means, through thought, of denoting the soul's innate strength. To forcibly place a restraint upon the expansion of the mind by limiting its content to a narrow and restricted path worketh a profound hardship. The law of Nature, which

is the Supreme Will expressed, demandeth that throughout the entire existence in physical form the soul through
the impulse of thought give evidence of an ever-increasing radius; that it, in the various fields of experience,
widen its horizon, versatility giving to speech the fragrance of a diversified knowledge. To, in the floral kingdom, delete all but one type of manifestation, would
be to impose a monotony which would weary inexpressibly the senses. Thus the restricted mind, through its
monotony, imposeth the content of a barren field of
thought. He who in versatile expression giveth evidence
of a normal expansion hath in intellectual pursuit fol-
lowed the path of the soul's unfoldment.

Propinquity lendeth to soul the incentive for comparative issue. It produceth an example on which to
pattern. Whether this be of an advantageous or a destructive nature dependeth on the model represented.
Propinquity through magnetic affiliation supplieth the
incentive for effort. The reason for thus impelling various group-souls to function lieth in the experience
the association affords. Only through experience doth
unfoldment take place, soul through the tincture of
disappointment, disillusionment, with the ever-accom-
panying bitterness of defeat, taking cognizance of the
reason involved. Within the most trivial circumstance
lieth a reason. Naught taketh place of happenstance.
From a minor and apparently inconsequential occurrence grave tragedies materialize, which may involve
a group or a nation in retaliatory measure. The initial
grain of sand formeth the base of the mighty strand, its
potential strength manifest in unity. Thus circumstance,
through the fragments of inconsequential occurrence,
buildeth the condition for an international discord. To
underestimate the trivial occurrence, relegating it to

the sphere of happenstance, is to denote a profund ignorance of the laws which govern the soul's evolution.

The concept of religion affordeth the basis for conclusion of the origin of being. It accepteth the Supreme God as the power omnipotent. It instinctively giveth homage to this, the Supreme Force. Soul may in denial refute the existence thereof until through bitter anguish it realizeth its manifold deficiency. The Omnipotent God formeth the source of the soul's derivation. This fact established, soul turneth to the demonstration of control. Through the mediatorship of the Christic Being is control superimposed, this being the source of the healing propensity, the love exemplified permeating the universe. The Christic Spirit this may truly be termed. Through innumerable channels of control is the universal principle exemplified. Radiating from the superlative heights, through the channel of thought is perpetuated the expression of the Divine. Thought is the means through which the Supreme Being demonstrateth control, it being the essence of the Divine. The cosmic universe, being in reality His power made manifest, is sustained through this, the force immeasurable. Throughout the universal kingdom Master Beings thus interpret the Supreme Will, functioning under the irrevocable control selflessness affords. Mediatorship denoteth the ever-present factor of supervision. Thought is the cosmic expression of the Divine, finding its source in the realm of interpretative being, radiated throughout the infinitude of space in varying degrees of strength and profundity, each soul being receptive thereto according to the stage of evolution in which it functions. The Supreme Will thus is expressed, that through the process evolution affords the ultimate of selfless being become an actuality.

Oracle Forty-Six

If a soul, which functions through the auspices the physical organism affords, centereth its yearning on the acquisition of material treasure it buildeth that which hath not permanent value. It buildeth a temple whose construction denoteth naught of stability. Founded on the material requisite, it subject is to change. Adverse condition may cause the foundation to crumble, to disintegrate, causing a collapse of the structure which involves an entire existence spent in the accumulation, the amassing thereof, when through transition soul passeth into the Great Beyond, the realm of shadowy unreality to the material mind, the realm of reality to the advanced and thinking soul who placeth upon material treasure the value of transient acquisition.

When, through the Portals of the Infinite, soul entereth the spiritual antithesis of physical being, what hath it with which to enhance? It leaveth all that it hath accomplished to enrich or impoverish humanity, as it may be, dependent on its ultimate use. Soul taketh with it as its inherent achievement but the dregs of experience, which through the comprehensive analysis that the Law requires prove of alloy, bitter to the taste. The draught of its own brewing must perforce be drained, that soul realize to the full the scope of its recent efforts. It seeth the extent of its influence. It traceth each thread of contact to the object of its proximity. It through remorse and comprehension buildeth anew the weakened fibre of the morale. If a man gain the whole world and lose his own soul, what hath he? Jesus the Master speaketh to humanity thus. He showeth the ultimate. He illumineth the path, whose narrow outline permits not of deviation. Soul in retrospection vieweth the fruits of its activities. It seeth all as on a vast scroll. If it hath made not an advance in the existence but completed, it prepareth to return for additional experience, to rebuild that which it hath unremittingly torn down. To realize that the law of karmic delineation requireth soul to, in consistent growth, expand; that growth must keep pace with a normal unfoldment; this alone if fully comprehended teacheth soul the futility of error. None escapes the Law. For, vigilant, it maintaineth a record of the individual soul, tabulating each thought, each act, according to its intrinsic worth.

Through the centuries past various interpretations have been released that humanity live within the tenets imposed. According to the generation involved hath been the teaching bestowed. Progress demandeth an advance in thought, in understanding. The archaic principle of surpassing loveliness must needs, through the spiritual analysis, be interpreted that the mass-mind take cognizance of the supervision maintained. It, through retrogression, denoteth a retarded condition. It maketh not an advance. It taketh backward the soul, making the descent, impelled by the urge of materialistic desire, by the backwash of experience. Motivated by selfish purpose which demandeth expression, humanity hath builded a debt of a supreme calibre, which causeth the Law to operate that it take cognizance of its innate weakness. Scant measure of the spiritual impulse motivates the mass-mind, which turneth with increasing yearning to indulgence. Man worketh not with but against his brother. He taketh; nor shareth. He woundeth; nor pauseth to heal with the essence of compassion. He seeth not the need, his eyes blinded by the glamour of selfish desire. He who liveth for the self, who seeketh not in alleviation to aid, buildeth that which bringeth pain, disillusionment, remorse. The Law, irrevocable, worketh with the precision the Supreme Will demands. These words pregnant are with meaning. He who worketh within the Law buildeth that which eternal is. He who abideth without maketh that which, when adversity stingeth, shall crumble and fall, leaving soul parched and dry on the oasis of despair.

Compassion delineateth the divine instinct. It seeketh to alleviate, to stem the tide of woe which as a mighty current sweepeth over a soul or a race, as it may be. It, through understanding, knoweth that within all lieth a purpose; that man hath builded that which torments, reaping but the result of his own efforts. According to the seed must the harvest be. He who planteth a thorn must from his own soul pluck its barb. He who placeth within the soil of life the seed of truth findeth his soul immeasurably enriched. He who maketh of gold his god findeth the metal of his idol tarnished, denoting but the dross of his yearning. He who in cruelty beateth to the earth the ripened grain findeth but the empty husks with which to replenish his store. The garden of the soul respondeth to the cultivation imposed. It groweth flowers of rare loveliness or the rank weeds of selfishness give forth the aroma of an adverse growth. Whatever the seed implanted, thus must the harvest denote its content, its worth. Man in selfish desire turneth to indulgence. He gratifieth the senses, giving to desire free rein. Folly leadeth, luring with the false echo of despair. Man taketh not heed, thinking to retrace his path when he hath through indulgence found surcease for his yearning. Knowest thou the cost of indulgence? That which teareth to shreds resistance, which of the morale maketh a weakened fibre, lendeth to soul not that which sustaineth. It is as a broken staff which lendeth not support. The reed which bendeth supporteth not when adversity

thrusteth upon soul a burden. It offereth not resistance
when the harsh tempest of remorse beateth soul relentlessly with the drenching torrent of sorrow. That which
alone sustaineth, supporteth, when life bruiseth is the
faith through which soul glimpseth the Divine, the all-
sustaining faith which assurance giveth of the eternal
Light. He who seeketh the Light dwelleth not within
the darkness, for he knoweth the darkness to be but the
shadow which fadeth into the oblivion of a decadent disbelief.

When Jesus spoke the promise of ancient delineation—seek and ye shall find—He in reality gave to humanity the key which openeth the portals of understanding. He who yearns turneth to the source of the Divine.
He in thought approacheth the Shrine of Universal
Being. Immersed within the Living Waters, soul in
unfoldment maketh the advance. Herein lieth the interpretation of these sacred words. Ever doth soul receive response when it calleth. As a light flasheth, doth
the Guiding Force respond, giving to soul the necessary
strength to sustain effort. No soul findeth the burden
insupportable. For when it weigheth past endurance
soul crieth aloud, seeking surcease. Thus the Law worketh, soul taking cognizance of its need. He who seeketh
finds the Mecca of his yearning. Soul seeketh that which
sustains. With an ever-increasing fervor it turneth to
the Divine when Spirit, through increased impetus,
supplieth effort. Thus unfoldment taketh place. The
Guiding Force giveth that which is as a beacon of light,
which illumineth for soul the path in advance. Soul
receiveth the Light; not that which blindeth, revealing
in its entirety the path, but that which softly illumines;
the Light which soul through its present understanding
comprehendeth. The seeker findeth his soul's desire
when it denoteth the treasure of the Spirit.

Oracle Forty-Seven

Thought is the invisible, intangible, process through which communion is accomplished, the means through which soul expresseth its predominating desire. It giveth to soul the ability to formulate in speech or act its motive. Thought therefore is of necessity the means through which a soul functioning through the auspices the physical organism affords receiveth the response, be it from whatsoever source. Soul, buoyant, impresseth upon mind the necessity for compliance. Thus is brain, through the multiple nerve-centers, an obedient agent. This delineates the physical process of achievement. The discarnate being, if he function within the astral delineation, through the means of concentration formeth an affiliation with a mind whose status denotes a similar or near stage of evolution, thought reaching the source of its objective. This may be of a mediocre or of an adverse nature, depending upon the stage of growth encompassed. The Immortal who through purification hath disbursed the consciousness of its complement, mind, functioning with the ease the spiritual status affords, through the perceptive ability penetrates the ether, focussing his concentrative effort on whatsoever objective his soul desireth to analyze. Perception is the spiritual awareness of the surrounding ether. It knoweth not limitation, for space existeth within that upon which the mind sets a limitation. Thought, the silent voice of the soul, through the concentrative ability reacheth the source of its objective, the spiritual strength delineating the force with which it is impelled.

Universality affordeth the interpretation through which soul hath discarded the restriction which creed imposeth, creed being the barrier which restricts

thought to a chosen area or limit. Universality embraceth the diversified field of exploration. It accepteth truth
as the basic foundation of all existent philosophies. It
taketh the element of spirituality, withdrawing the varying folds which illusion and glamour provide, and in
concentrative analysis permeates its depth. It discardeth
caste as a barrier to growth, basing its estimate on the
stage of evolution in which the soul in question functions. It seeth the divine element as the connecting link
between all existent souls, glimpsing the weakness manifest with the compassion understanding affords. It seeth
each stage of progress as necessary in the cycle evolution
provides. It looketh at the various planes of consciousness, delineating a less advanced status, with the clear
vision which embraces likewise the superlative planes to
which it, through preordination, aspires. Glimpsing
its own deficiency, soul maketh comparison with the
advanced, even as it seeth the less advanced stage of
growth. Universal the concept of religion and all that
it embraceth.

Universality is the supreme ideal to which each soul
must aspire. Color, the line which separateth the Caucasian from the Mongolian, the Ethiopian from the
Indian, becometh non-existent. For the spiritual vision
embraceth these, the various races, as delineating individual grades in the vast school of experience, the predominating color exemplifying the exact grade in which
soul in the present existence functions. Civilization imposeth a barrier which for social and economic means
barreth inter-marriage. But the spiritual essence through
which being is motivated provideth the identical course
in each and every channel of activity. The barrier of
color must in the ultimate merge within the final analysis
which accepteth all and denieth none.

Experience giveth to each soul the exact stage in which growth is assured. Retrogression at various eras retardeth the advance, thrusting upon soul the backwash of experience, soul thus being forced to take cognizance of its inherent and predominating weakness. Thus is comprehension taken of the futility of error. And soul, when it hath digested the fruits of experience, through the process rebirth affords maketh an advance. Naught is happenstance, each act of trivial consequence delineating a purpose. Soul through experience widens its scope, its perspective, growth providing the means for expansion. On whatsoever plane soul functions it receiveth that which meets its immediate need, acceptance being the irrevocable law of control. Sorrow, pain, joy, bliss—these are the factors through which soul expresseth the varying emotions which experience provides.

The Immortal whose understanding precludeth censure, condemnation, whose vision embraces evolution in its entirety, knoweth the bliss of communion in a superlative degree, the compensating peace giving to soul the impetus for an ever-increasing effort. The varying emotions, which a supreme content induces, create a compassion so profound that the desire for alleviation is the predominating characteristic. Service provideth the outlet for activity. Thus the Immortal through service exemplifieth the Law, control being the measure of restraint pertaining to all grades of evolution, both physical and etheric. Supervision provideth the channel through which the Immortal, be it on whatsoever plane of consciousness, serveth. To realize that each object in existence is subject to control from a superior force, that naught operates as a free agent, tends to create a sense of responsibility. The example set hath a profound significance, as through comparative issue it formeth the pattern for one in a less advanced stage. If it be up-lifting, idealistic, it is as a light which illumines. If it be of an adverse character it is as a shadow which dimmeth the light. The responsibility is apparent. Prox-imity formeth the ever-present factor of incentive, soul through the imitative ability patterning on that which intrigues, with a desire for a like achievement. He, who through a painstaking and constant supervision of thought regulates the soul's activities to the channel of constructive effort, setteth an example which brings to the soul involved the steady growth consistent with progress.

The physical universe giveth soul the opportunity for diversified experience, soul through the auspices of the flesh lending itself to the delineation the varying emotions embrace; desire, lust, passion, being the means through which the propagative instinct is impelled and fostered. These form the nucleus of the sex-urge, mag-netic affinity being the means through which gravitation, one to another, taketh place. Cosmic the affiliation as is all that existeth, the cosmic universe delineating the operative will of the supreme and omnipotent God. Desire formeth the means through which unity taketh place, superinduced through the mating impulse. Here-in lieth the source of creature ills; disease, disability, being the active result of abuse of this, Nature's law for propagation.

Man useth not the divine instruments through which birth is established for constructive effort. Through indulgence he gratifieth the senses, thereby thrusting upon the physical organism a hardship. The vital es-sence, transmuted within the channel of intellectual pursuit, lendeth brilliancy to the mind. It giveth to soul a freedom of expression it knoweth not when through indulgence it lendeth mind to the gratification of the lower senses. Therein lieth the source of mental unrest. Mind through perverse disobedience centereth its yearning, not on that which uplifts, but on that which debases thought. The stream denoteth its content, scintillating with crystal-clearness or murky, discolored, with the debris of impure desire. The unclean mind repels with the disbursing of its predominating desire. It reflecteth as in a mirror the debasing content. To, in thought, castigate mind, forcing it to center its yearning on that which uplifts, which enriches, is to curb its activity in a degenerative channel. Birth is the divine process of reproduction. It must of necessity be impelled, motivated, by desire. To analyze the motive for the act involved is to place it in the category of perverse or constructive effort.

When upon humanity the law of rebirth bestowed the process through which the propagating of the species taketh place, it gave to the individual soul the varying grades which temptation embraces. Love, tenderness, divinity—all are embodied in this which soul expresseth in its visitation to the physical universe. Love, which motivates in unselfish desire, embraces, heals, lifts the companionate member; striving to, through alleviation, give to soul a protection which sustains. This typifies love which finds its source in the kinship of soul, which knoweth not separation. Love which bruises, which inflicts on its companionate member a hardship, is that which through its impermanency may be designated as an affiliation of the flesh. The material mind comprehendeth not the reason for abstinence, being in that stage of evolution where indulgence is the means through which soul satisfieth desire. The flame which through its intensity denoteth an impermanency burneth to extinction, leaving but the embers which are as the ashes of disillusionment. Periodic the union thus established, each connection but bruising soul with its futile effort for fulfilment. Desire thrusteth a hardship upon soul at this stage of evolution. Within it must the lesson of self-control, of the strengthening of the will, be taught. Soul must through denial, renunciation, force mind to compliance. It must castigate thought, forcing it from the channel of a profound self-indulgence to the course of constructive effort. Dalliance but prolongeth the inevitable.

Oracle Forty-Eight

Jesus in physical being sought to bestow upon humanity an ideal of priceless beauty. Giving of His bounty in generous measure, withholding naught which through its essence might inspire to like pattern, He in unselfish purpose served. Descending through the dictum of the Supreme Intelligence, whose will is omnipotent, He in service exemplified that obedience which knoweth no equal. Each existent soul must in a profound humility accept this pattern of selflessness as the supreme ideal on which to mold the soul-structure. Heir to the weakness desire imposeth, temptation thrusts upon soul the means of gratification. The will must through innate strength refusal give. Habit must through constant supervision train mind, exacting that obedience which knoweth no deviation. Herein lieth the key to unfoldment. Mind denoteth a tenacity which in repetition thrusts upon soul the urge for indulgence. Only through a rigid, unrelenting, supervision doth mind lend itself to control. Thought being the means through which soul expresseth its innate desire, it must of necessity operate in active delineation through the auspices of the mind. Herein lieth the difficulty. Mind as an independent organ serveth soul, extracting from the consciousness that which through its irrelevancy hath no bearing on soul's insistence. Mind weaveth into wierd patterns this, the essence of desire, as represented in the dregs of experience. Insanity thus delineates the activity of mind, with soul, its supervising intelligence, withdrawn. To recognize the intricate and delicate process through which mind, the complement of soul, operateth is to in a measure more deeply comprehend the necessity for a surveillance which is unremitting.

Unfoldment formeth the process through which enlightenment becometh an active factor. Imperceptibly soul respondeth to the love-essence which permeates. It, through a gradually increasing strength, taketh cognizance of the Divine, turning to this, the source of being, drawn as by a magnet of supreme power. For this exemplifieth the Father's love, which depthless, measureless, is. Thus soul, through the magnetic essence, is drawn to the Divine, releasing by imperceptible degrees its yearning for that which debaseth, replacing with that which through its unselfish note uplifts. Soul casteth off the fetters of materialistic aspiration, basing its valuation on that which imperishable is. It seeth humanity with its frailty, its weakness, revealed as a vast generation whose various activities denote the process of transmutation through which the dross becometh the purified essence. Thus compassion replaceth condemnation. Love enfoldeth hatred. Gradual as the coming of the dawn is this, the birth of understanding, it representing the dawning of the eternal Light. Enlightenment provideth the process through which soul in communion within the Silence formeth a unity with the Divine Mind, becoming an active part thereof.

Love, compassion and charity form the divine elements of understanding. These are the attributes of the selfless soul, the active principles through which soul, having made the ascent to the immortal heights, in service exemplifieth the Law. Love reflecteth the divine instinct, the all-embracing healing essence, it being the direct unity with the Divine Mind which affords the supply from which soul draweth its content. Love, all-forgiving, seeth not the predominating weakness. It centereth its concentration on the element of divinity, which motivateth soul. Thus it censureth, condemneth, not. This exemplifieth love. Compassion denoteth the healing essence of love, it being given birth through understanding. Healing, it enwrappeth, seeking in alleviation to lift the burden of pain which weigheth inexpressibly the object of its ministration. It expresseth the Divine, being the outward manifestation thereof. Charity is the means through which love expresseth. It giveth tenderly, rejoicing in the privilege. It bestoweth the Bread of Life, which alone satisfieth, which giveth to the down-trodden, the suffering, the courage with which to once again lift the burden of woe, the cross of its own building. For only thus doth suffering overwhelm the soul. It is the accumulated debt which soul disburseth through bodily pain, mental unrest and distress, with an accompanying anguish. Only thus soul taketh cognizance of its innate and predominating weakness. Charity giveth in love, exemplifying the generosity which asketh naught in return.

Love, understanding, compassion, charity—these are the priceless jewels of divinity, the gems with which soul adorneth the consciousness, which through their gleaming radiance denote the selfless state of being. It was this the Master Jesus bestowed on humanity, that through the supreme sacrifice it glimpse the Divine. It is to this each soul must aspire as the ultimate. It is the diadem of light which replaceth the crown of thorns which each soul weareth until, through renunciation, it hath cast aside selfish desire.

Oracle Forty-Nine

Behold, the Living Word poureth forth that humanity take cognizance of the living Christ. From the celestial heights speaketh the Voice which bringeth a message of peace, of good-will to man. Love thou one another. Love it is which giveth to soul the ability to succor, to aid, to lift the burden which through its weight crusheth the weary soul. Love it is which healeth with the essence of divine compassion; which soothes, giving to soul renewed courage with which to withstand the fret of the physical existence. Love imperishable, eternal, is. It knoweth naught of fluctuation; its strength intensified through the understanding manifest. He who giveth in love knoweth the joy of rewarded effort. Love alone showeth the way to the Cross upon whose rugged frame each soul must crucify the material instinct, the selfish purpose through which soul turneth the ear deaf to the suffering of humanity. Love illumineth the path to peace. If a man knoweth not love his soul of evil propensity is. For even as love breatheth of divinity, so its absence denoteth the error of thought through which soul glimpseth not the Divine.

Hatred findeth its birth in selfish purpose. Of retaliatory measure, it seeketh to wound the adversary. He who woundeth shall in turn experience the anguish of the piercèd soul. He shall receive in proportion to that which he hath bestowed. Therefore, Beloved, take thou heed of these the words of the Master, who speaketh unto thee. Love alone it is which shall sustain, giving to thee the necessary strength with which to withstand defeat.

Oracle Fifty

Whyfore have I come unto thee, Beloved? It is that thou mayest take heed of these, my words. Dark the path through which thou art traversing the desert of experience. Knowest thou the reason for this, the darkness of the mind? Thou hast dimmed the Light of understanding, the flame through which Spirit urgeth man to the completement of his task. This, the divine flame, burneth dimly, giving to soul the opaque and darkened lens through which it glimpseth not the purpose of its being. The Supreme Father it is who hath ordained the individual soul traverse the cycle of evolution to its ultimate achievement. In His infinite wisdom, which depthless is, He hath created the individual soul in the likeness of His own image. Divine the concept; for thus He exemplifieth the Law, which irrevocable is. He createth the infinite spark which through preordination shall illumine the soul-structure, permeating its substance, reflecting the essence of His love. Man knoweth not the ultimate. He seeth but a brief distance in advance. Soul through the urge of Spirit respondeth with increasing intensity, delineating the working of the Law. The Law is the Word, in which lieth control, this being the means through which evolution taketh place. The Law worketh to fulfilment. He who liveth therein knoweth not fear. For the phantoms of darkness, which are of the mind, walk but with the oppressed whose faith burneth dimly. Therefore I say unto thee: he who walketh in love knoweth but peace, which is the divine robe with which soul encaseth its being.

Knowest thou the reason for the darkness which as a pall obscureth the sun of love from the mass-mind, from humanity at large? The reason lieth in the selfish desire

which permeateth, which impels soul in the spirit of
greed to wrest from another, a weaker member, his
daily bread. He who taketh loseth in like manner. Canst
thou not vision this, the working of the Law? Take thou
heed, Beloved. Seek within the effect the cause of this
which distresseth. Thou knowest the suffering, the yearning. Thou seest the needy, the halt, the lame which surround thee. Thy heart respondeth not with pity. Immersed in thy selfishness, thou art deaf to the cry, the
plea, of thy needy brother. Thou canst not make the
advance until thou vision with compassion him who
suffers. The soul which turneth away knoweth not the
compassion which healeth, which bruiseth not. It taketh; nor giveth in return. The orthodox mind closeth
its portals to the need of humanity. It seeth but the narrow path its creed outlines. It goeth not into the hidden
byways to alleviate. Suffering lieth in all paths of progress. It existeth in the high and in the lowly. It speaketh
of the hunger of the body and of the mind, the thirst of
the soul which craveth the elixir of spiritual interpretation. Hunger parcheth with the essence of despair. It
createth a dreary waste which soul crosseth, moaning
with pain. Canst thou not pattern thy effort on that
which was the superlative example? He who through the
crucifixion delineated the Father's will denied none
who sought His presence. Freely He gave of His bounty.
He through compassion segregated not the needy.
Wherefore hast thou denied thy brother who knoweth
not thy faith? Thou didst emerge equal in soul. Thou
shalt in the ultimate cast aside thy prejudice as that
which disrupts growth. Each soul hath within it the
divine element. This establisheth brotherhood. Caste is
but the selfish armour in which the adolescent soul encaseth its being. Love dissolveth caste. It dissipateth as

the mist before the sun. Thou who erectest a barrier of caste, which barreth from another soul thy compassion, shall in return experience the pain of the denial thou art inflicting. He who oppresseth shall in turn know oppression. The manifestation of love it is which is the key which openeth the portals to unfoldment. If man make not progress in spiritual growth; if he dally, but encrusting soul more deeply with the barnacles of selfishness, he cometh again into physical being to, through reversal, taste the dregs of bitterness. The Law demandeth the soul through unfoldment take cognizance of the Divine. If it turneth away, refusing to glimpse the Light, it through the oppression of frustrated desire reversal maketh; seeking, groping for that which alleviates.

Oracle Fifty-One

Cast from thee the false interpretation of creed. Permit thy yearning, thy love, to extend its tendrils, embracing those who suffer. Universal must be thy understanding, embracing that which breathes of truth. Turn from that which constricts, which bindeth thee. The Supreme God to whom thy soul turneth in homage is thy all in all. It is to Him thou must turn, for therein lieth thy strength. To the supreme mediator, Jesus the Christ, must thou in supplication seek for thy soul's sustenance. He it is who reacheth forth in love immeasurable to solace, to give. His healing power is manifest to the soul who in unselfish purpose lifteth its silent plea. Immeasurable, depthless, the content of His love, His compassion. Thou who art yearning, seeking, who glimpse but the shadow of the Light, turn from that which blindeth thee. It is thy desire which permitteth not thy soul to, in clarity, vision the Divine. Purify thy desire. Probe within its depth. There wilt thou find the source of thy weakness. Again thy Elder Brother speaketh in terms of love. If thou lovest thou canst not wound. Love precludes that which bruiseth. Therefore if within thy soul lieth not love, therein lieth the source of thy deficiency. Within the Holy Word is exemplified the Law. This Law I give unto thee. Within it are the requisites of growth, the irrevocable law of eternal consequence. Until thou hast conquered the self; until thou canst vision all who err in love, in understanding, in compassion, thou canst not enter the Kingdom of the Blest. Love, imperishable, eternal, alone giveth to soul the peace which passeth understanding.

Oracle Fifty-Two

Blessed is the peace-maker. What meaneth these words? Within their content lieth that which worketh for good. He who poureth the oil of understanding upon the troubled waters of human endeavor is a builder of the vast empire of the soul. In divine understanding, he giveth of the essence of love. Humanity knoweth not the peace of a tranquil existence. It pursueth that which lures with the false promise of fulfilment. It centereth its yearning on the acquisition of material gain, that which perishable is when the harsh wind of adversity bloweth. As the sand it crumbles, the foundation of the soul denoting its faulty construction. What availeth it if man build that whose permanency is as naught. The ashes of defeat replace the living embers of hope. Thus worketh the Law. It apportions to each soul the fruits of the harvest. If but the empty husks remain, it denoteth the drought of a selfish desire. If man implant within the soil of life that which beareth fruit, it of necessity giveth forth of like content. The thorn beareth a thorn as progeny. The lily bringeth into being the replica of its purity. Man planteth within the soil the barbed and poisoned thorn of hatred; it multiplieth into vast proportion. It, fanned by the breeze of an adverse yearning, scattereth its petals throughout space, impregnating the virgin soil where heretofore naught gave evidence of being. Herein lieth a responsibility of vast proportion. The thorn which multiplieth through its intensity of strength denoteth the evil content of the mass-thought. Hatred, greed, lust—these, the thorns of evil propensity, impregnate the soil of universal thought throughout the physical plane of activity. As a monstrous blight it crusheth the spiritual foundation of being. Wherein lieth the curative measure?

Suffering giveth to soul the necessity for a reversal. Soul in the extremity of a physical or a mental anguish seeketh within the effect the cause. The Master-Surgeon, with the divine compassion which understanding bestows, cauterizeth that the healing essence become apparent. Man singeth with joy when the innate and predominating desire knoweth appeasement. If it be adverse it teareth apart the morale. If it be that which rewards constructive effort it giveth a compensating peace. Whatsoever be the desire, it must needs be frustrated that man take cognizance of its import. The spiritual unfoldment giveth evidence of a cessation of activity. Soul when necessity demands entereth into the tranquil calm of suspended growth. Herein lieth the working of a law. It through sustained tranquillity becometh stabilized, strengthened. It in retrospection scanneth the thread of the fabric of the soul, noting its innate strength. It through comprehension reneweth the effort for unfoldment when soul, inactive, demandeth expression. The Law worketh twofold. The soul who in selfish desire indulgeth the self, through satiation, accompanied by a profound remorse, taketh cognizance of the futility of error. Thus the crime which halteth the criminal activity, this being the accumulation of an adverse effort which through a protracted period hath builded a debt of supreme magnitude. None escape the Law; it worketh irrevocably.

Oracle Fifty-Three

Come unto Me, thou who suffer, and I will lift thy burden. Thus spake Jesus. Within these words lieth a promise which worketh within the Law. All that existeth in tangible and intangible manifestation denoteth control, the Supreme Will being thus delineated. He who seeketh in love, in humility, with naught of selfish purpose, receiveth the balm of a profound and sustaining peace. The soul through its resignation hath earned this gracious privilege. It approacheth the shrine of the Divine, receptive through the subjugation of desire, to the healing inflow. It centereth its yearning on the spiritual, the pure. Thus it receiveth in proportion to the need manifest. He who maketh supplication with the will in opposition to the Divine, who crieth for surcease, giving naught in return, heareth but the echo of his yearning. For the portal of Divine Comprehension embraces but the supplicant who seeketh in humility, in obedience to the Divine Will. Man in the extremity of mental anguish, imposed when sorrow thrusteth the cruel blade of loss within the citadel of the heart, demandeth surcease, turning instinctively to the source of the Divine. He hath demanded entrance, casting not aside that which sealeth the portal. He knocketh, clinging to the barrier that he hath erected, which barreth entrance. Knowest thou the reason for the refusal? Soul must through self-denial, through resignation to the Divine Will, acknowledge its weakness; must through yearning for the Divine build anew the structure weakened through self-indulgence. Compassionate, infinitely tender, the Guiding Force which apportions to each soul that which fosters growth. He who turneth in love, seeking alleviation of his pain, receiveth in proportion to the faith manifest. If he hath earned a surcease through comprehension of error the Law worketh, giving that which strengthens, with a compensating peace. He who hath signified his worthiness entereth the sacred precincts of the Divine, drinking from the Living Waters.

Man crieth aloud in his sorrow. Thus is resistance weakened. He accepteth according to his understanding. He seeth the companionate soul maketh the advance when through transition it from physical to spiritual changeth its activity. He accepteth that which hath been imposed, seeing Death as an angel in disguise. He recognizeth the summons as the advance to activity on a higher and broader plane of consciousness. Bitterness formeth not a part. For the resignation to the Divine Will precludeth resistance. Man knoweth not the hour when the summons cometh. If his task be incomplete he must perforce return again to, in physical delineation, undergo the identical experience. If through constructive effort he hath builded that which denotes perfected workmanship he maketh the advance, accepting the summons in the sustained faith understanding provides. Each soul respondeth according to its faith, seeing transition as the portal which admits soul to the realm of a spiritual interpretation of effort, with a corresponding reward for achievement.

Oracle Fifty-Four

The Living Word poureth forth that humanity take heed of the call. He who dallies, who in procrastination retards his soul's progress, knoweth the aftermath of defeated purpose. That on which he concentrates his yearning shall be as Dead Sea fruit, parching the soul with its bitter essence. Thus the backwash of experience bestows that which cauterizeth soul of its predominating weakness. He who with blinded vision seeth not the working of the Law is as one who, with faltering steps, approacheth the precipice with naught of protective measure. It availeth naught. For within the consciousness lieth that which must be eradicated before to soul cometh the ability to vision with clarity the law of eternal consequence. He who turneth from the Light must of necessity traverse the darkened plane of a pronounced disbelief. For even as the Light the reverse is of darkness, so is faith that which opposeth disbelief. Whence cometh the Light? It is the Father's love made manifest. It is the all-pervading, the omnipresent, the beatific essence of divinity which permeateth the soul that receptive is. It knoweth naught of limitation. It embraceth with the healing element of a divine comprehension, depthless, immeasurable. Thus is interpreted that which man knoweth as the Light. Eternal, it fluctuateth not. Illuminative, it maketh of the darkness a negligible quantity. It maketh of soul a Temple from which the divine essence casteth its radiance, illumining for those who walk in the darkness of the mind the path to fulfilment. If thou dimmest thy Light, fearful of the shafts of antagonism, of censure, which with rapier sharpness pierce thy consciousness, thou art breaking the Law. For it readeth that he who knoweth the joy of divine communion, who hath sensed within his soul the all-pervading peace of a unity with the Divine, through the lighting of the path for another soul enricheth immeasurably the self. The Law giveth in reward for compassionate effort and it depleteth for the infringement of a spiritual tenet. If thou withholdest thine own Light, causing thy brother to falter, to bruise the soul because of thy delinquency, thou hast builded a debt which must of necessity be obviated. Therefore, Beloved, within this, the law of compassionate instinct, lieth that which must of necessity impel thee. Thou art that which the Father hath ordained shouldst through evolution become a pure, a selfless, soul. The return to Spirit must of necessity be accomplished, that thou mayest serve; that in unity thou mayest demonstrate the laws through which supervision, control, is established. Thou knowest naught of choice, for the ultimate is that which the Supreme Will ordaineth. Man in his puny strength defieth this, the Omnipotent Will. As to a babe, the Guiding Force giveth that through which shall comprehension dawn of the futility of error, and refusal of compliance. He who addresseth thee, tender, compassionate, seeketh to instill within thee the yearning for obedience, for acceptance of this, the law of spiritual delineation. He seeketh to illumine for thee the path to fulfilment. He calleth that thou mayest hear with clarity the Voice. He cometh in Living Thought to make known His presence. Thou didst accept in its entirety the sacrament of the crucifixion, apportioning to a risen Christ the ascent, the transfiguration. What meaneth these words, Beloved? The transfiguration is that which through its radiance illumines. It maketh clear that which is. All-embracing, illuminative, it knoweth naught to darken the horizon. Thus the Master Jesus speaketh to humanity.

The Living Thought which floweth forth through the channel of instrumentation giveth to humanity the laws of unfoldment. It denieth to none the privilege of communion. He who will may enter the Holy Presence if he cleanse the soul of selfish desire, making supplication with yearning for a closer unity with the Divine. Thus the Father ordaineth. He who seeketh shall find; shall drink from the Living Waters when soul, parched, in resignation to the Supreme Will, approacheth in humility the shrine of the Divine. The scoffer knoweth not the joy of communion. The peace which passeth understanding permeateth not the content of his consciousness. He through denial erecteth the barrier which insurpassable is, which denieth entrance to the holy inflow. With compassionate instinct regard this, the adolescence of spiritual understanding. For even as the slender reed becometh through growth the mighty tree, so must the unbelieving soul through unfoldment mature into that which embraceth the divine truth of spiritual analysis. The scoffer woundeth but the self. For, ever doth the shaft of prejudice rebound, piercing the consciousness of him who hath with arrow of hatred striven to bruise the faith of the believer. The law through which unfoldment taketh place giveth impartially to the soul that which it hath earned: the compensating peace of constructive effort or the dregs of bitterness for adverse achievement.

Oracle Fifty-Five

Beloved, I would that thou shouldst pay heed to these, my words. Causation is the operative law through which the effect becometh manifest. If thou speak in wrath thou of necessity placest the barb of an antagonistic regard within the soul of the recipient. If thou speak in love, thy tenderness apparent, thou likewise hast implanted the seed of compassion. The incipient seed with which thou hast impregnated the soil of humanity taketh root. It matureth, bearing the fruit of its incipient being. It multiplieth. If it be the dank weed of an adverse thought it, through the multiple process, maketh a harvest of vast proportion. If it be a flower of spiritual significance its fragile loveliness must needs be nurtured with tenderness. Whatsoever be the seed, determineth the harvest. Thus is hatred made manifest, cruelty being the blade with which the consciousness is pierced. If man give forth from the depth of his understanding but love it formeth a shield which protects the soul, which maketh of soul an impregnable power through which the Divine Will operateth. According to the channel doth the stream flow. It is as a torrent which through deficient control sweepeth the debris of adverse effort in destructive measure. Or as a river, whose depth determines its strength, it floweth in harmonious accord. Thou mayest determine the innate strength of the soul through the control manifest. He who through control giveth an example of strength is a power through which nations are swayed. He who through weakness vacillates denoteth that through which destruction taketh place. The Law worketh twofold. Power misused carrieth in its wake disaster. Power directed within the channel of constructive effort buildeth the empire of eternal significance. Thou mayest bear aloft the torch of Light or trail the banner of defeat according to thy innate desire. Desire maketh of man a slave. If he indulgence give he knoweth not the liberty of a free choice, for desire demonstrateth satisfaction. If he cauterize desire, forcing to constructive effort its urge, he maketh of desire a slave in bondage. Seest thou the necessity for control? In thought lieth the necessity for discipline. For thought it is which giveth birth to speech, to act. Thought, the insidious means through which soul expresseth, alone maketh of man a power for good or a force of evil propensity. As a man thinketh, he is. Thus readeth the Law. The consciousness retaineth all that is imprinted therein. It recordeth with unfailing precision the content of thought. If thou couldst read this, thy soul's expression, scanning each line with the clear vision of understanding, thou wouldst bar entrance to that which beareth not the imprint of purity. Thus must soul when transition taketh place, with the veil lifted from memory, scan each thought, with its corresponding effect, in a comprehensive analysis segregating, retaining that which denoteth worth and discarding as waste that which through its impurity beareth the imprint of the adverse. Thus soul taketh cognizance of its predominating weakness, building anew that with which to further the existence which lieth in advance when, purged, it descendeth to through additional experience strengthen its resistance to defeat.

Oracle Fifty-Six

The Living Voice which speaketh cometh from the source of the Divine. It bringeth to humanity the requisites for spiritual unfoldment. It illumineth the path through which soul casteth aside the fetters which are as an insupportable burden, which weigh, forcing the mind within the channel of an indulgence disastrous to growth. The Living Voice, which is in reality the Word, cometh from the Master-Healer who, from the superlative heights, extendeth to humanity that compassion which heals, which lifteth soul, revealing the eternal Light. Thus alone soul glimpseth the ultimate, through the portals of the Divine, for there lieth that which each soul must attain. It must through renunciation take heed of the source whence was derived its being. Dalliance but prolongeth the cycle soul trends from incipient being to the ultimate achievement. Man denieth the Voice, relying on his own strength. What availeth denial? Sorrow, privation, mental distress, physical disability—these, the means through which cauterization taketh place, shatter the barrier soul hath builded through denial, exposing soul to the harsh wind of adverse content. Thus the Law worketh, administering the discipline through which soul reverseth its course, accepting the spiritual interpretation of being, casting aside the prejudice which hath provided the staff which lendeth support. Self-sufficient, soul becometh dependent, seeking in supplication for a surcease from defeat. The Law which forceth soul to compliance delineateth the Supreme Will operative through innumerable channels of control. Irrevocable the will imposed, it being the system the Supreme Intelligence ordaineth for the evolution through which the soul, free, becometh an instrument of supreme value. Unfoldment provideth the means through which growth becometh manifest. What meaneth this term? Unfoldment delineates the process through which the chrysalis soul becometh, through the casting aside of selfish desire, the radiant and selfless being. It is the transformation from the immature to the mature, from the adolescent to the intellectual state of being. Eons comprise that which maketh of soul a power for good, eons through which soul alternates from spiritual to physical interpretation of being, perpetuated by the process of rebirth. For thus alone is evolution fostered, rebirth being the supreme achievement of the Creator's art, impelled by the propagative instinct which fosters creation. Thus worketh the law of control.

Oracle Fifty-Seven

Creation embraceth the universal principle. It formeth the foundation upon which the physical universe
rests. It, through spiritual delineation, embraceth the
replica of that which the soul manifesting in physical
being visions. It formeth the hypothesis on which mind
baseth its conclusion, its theory, be it of whatsoever
delineation. Therefore creation is all-encompassing,
comprising the universal principle. From the superlative heights is control demonstrated, the Omnipotent
Will impelling implicit obedience, be it from whatsoever factor. Thus is creation perpetuated. It embraceth
the universe, comprising all orbs which in the starry
firmament delight man with their scintillating brilliancy, each orb rotating in eternal continuity in the
particular groove or sphere its stage of evolution provides as applicable to progress. Thus the soul, be it of
whatsoever stage of growth, findeth in the physical universe the exact planet which its evolutionary status apportions as suitable to progress. A law worketh in
universal proportion which knoweth no deviation. The
scientist through the auspices of technical research seeketh to determine the exact position in space, visible from
the physical orb on which he functions. Limital the
exploration, the far reaches of space lending themselves
not to analysis therefrom. When to man cometh the
realization that the universal principle inexhaustible,
immeasurable, is; that the single existence is as but one
mosaic in the pattern of soul's continuity, the analysis
will be based, not on the material delineation, but the
spiritual analysis, which through its potent interpretation giveth the true conception of universal construction. The creative impulse impelleth soul in its orbit
of activity, be it of whatsoever exemplification. In spirit-

ual antithesis it, in concentrative effort, buildeth anew
the fabric of the soul that through the process of rebirth
it enter into physical interpretation with increased
stamina. It, through the supervision of the Guiding
Force, descendeth when the Law designates the period
applicable for individual experience. Love, the eternal,
the imperishable tie which uniteth one soul to another
fosters experience, providing the means of support, of
comparative issue, which impels effort.

Supply is that which giveth to soul the means of
sustenance. Be it of the spiritual manna or of the physical, the material, abundance, it is that which promotes
a state of well-being. It is that for which soul in a spirit
of greed, of rancour, extracteth from another his portion. In over-abundance it constitutes that which man
designateth as wealth, the spiritual interpretation of
wealth being the riches, the treasure, of the mind which
enhance thought, which imperishable are. Man committeth a crime that he may increase materially his supply. He exceedeth his need, amassing with the spirit of
greed that for which he hath not use. Thus is control
established, monopoly demonstrated. If the excess be
directed within the channel of a humanitarian project,
that which benefits humanity individually or at large,
it worketh for good. If it be forced within the channel
of constructive effort it uplifteth; is as an incentive to
progress. On the reverse, wealth diverted from the
channel of public benefit, wasted in selfish indulgence,
its surplus enriching but the individual benefiting therefrom—wealth thus employed bringeth to the soul involved a debt of supreme calibre. In the existence which
lieth in advance must the reversal take place, poverty
with the lash of physical disability teaching soul that
indulgence is but another exemplification of greed,

which findeth its birth in desire. Ever doth desire impel soul to effort. To trace the instinct of greed must the soul content be analyzed from the standpoint of desire. For desire alone it is which impelleth soul to action. To, in moments of doubt, scan the motive employed is to know for a certainty the source of its incipient being. Desire of an adverse character findeth its birth in selfish instinct. It centereth its yearning on that which indulgence provides. It thinketh not of another, being absorbed in that which pertaineth to the self. The Golden Adage readeth: man must do that which he would should be done unto him. No deviation existeth, it being the irrevocable law of karmic delineation, that to which soul must aspire. Thus brotherhood is established. When soul through cognizance of this, the divine tie, taketh heed of that to which it must attain, the fret, the adversity which try the endurance, bruising soul, will be transposed into a peace so profound, so all-embracing, that as a phantom of the mind will be these, the vicissitudes of physical endeavor; soul, illumined by Spirit, motivated by love, embracing all who err in the compassion of the profound understanding predominating.

Oracle Fifty-Eight

What maketh of soul a Temple? Soul a Temple becometh when through subservience of the will it giveth obeisance to the Divine. It through concentration renounceth worldly desire, the material instinct becoming that which centers its yearning on service, in whatsoever field the Guiding Force apportions as applicable to the soul's activity. It through resignation accepteth the Divine Will as omnipotent, supreme, dwelling within the tenets bestowed. Soul in homage lighteth the tapers of its faith before the altar of the Divine, the incense of its yearning becoming apparent. Thus soul, illumined by Spirit, the divine element, consecrateth the self to service. Service denoteth the yearning for the alleviation of those who suffer, who in privation await the summons through which cognizance is taken of the Divine. It is that through which the humanitarian instinct becometh apparent. It is the establishing of the tie of brotherhood, the universal link in the chain of eternal continuity, in which soul in a fervor of joy giveth of its all. The adolescent whose yearning is centered on the material experiences not this, the divine instinct. The soul-structure, opaque, reflecteth not the Spirit's radiance. Unfoldment, with the ever-recurring rebirth, bringeth this, the awareness of the Divine. Thus each soul through growth trends the path to understanding.

Thou, who art serving in filial fidelity, who hast renounced worldly desire, who through the awareness of the Divine seekest in yearning to draw closer to the shrine of thy being—listen to the words which He, the Master, speaketh. It is to thee these words are addressed. Serve thou in love, in compassion. Lift thou thy erring brother. Shield with the essence of thy love. Thou art as one, for the tie of divinity uniteth thee. Illumine the path that he who knoweth not thy peace may through its radiance glimpse the source. Tenderly must thou lead, thou who carriest the torch of the Infinite. Cast its gleam afar, that the ray of purity turn from the darkness of despair the oppressed, lighting the gloom of disbelief, dissipating the shadows, among which lurk the phantoms of superstition, of error. Thou art as a torch. Lest thy Light be dimmed wear thou the symbol of the Cross; that, protection giving, it shield thee from the barbed shafts of hatred, of antagonism, which ever beset the disciple of the Master. Thus the unbelieving seek to disarm purity, tearing to shreds the robe of divine comprehension with which the soul is encased. He who addresses thee seeth in humanity the divine element. He glimpseth the weakness, the weariness, of soul with compassion. He seeth the darkness of the mind which obscureth the Holy Light. He visions the ultimate which each soul must attain. He seeth the weary path which lieth in advance; the desert of arid waste through which soul must pass, drinking of the diversified content from the goblet Experience provides; the gleaming faith, mingled with the bitter dregs of disappointment, of defeat, of disillusionment, making of soul a harsh and brittle substance; to, through transmutation, become the purified element. Thy Elder Brother seeth all. Therefore He speaketh in words of wisdom. Thou who hast glimpsed the Light, within whose soul the all-pervading peace permeateth with the bliss of communion, of a unity with the Divine—through thy understanding make manifest the Supreme Will which motivateth thee. Give thou generously of thy bounty. The soul which parched with thirst knoweth not the satisfaction of plenty, must needs be nourished that the hunger be appeased. It must through compassionate instinct come into an awareness of its deficiency, its inherent and predominating weakness. By thy example thou mayest give to humanity the incentive for like effort. Therefore heed thou the words which thy Elder Brother speaketh. Permit thy Light to shine, that the shadows of the night become transformed into the gleaming radiance of the dawn, the new era in which man shall work with and not against his brother. Thus the Law readeth. He who wounds knoweth not love. For love, tender, compassionate, healeth. Canst thou ascend the Cross in resignation, accepting the Father's will? Each soul carrieth a Cross it hath builded through indulgence of desire. To lift its weight must soul in cognizance of its error turn to the source of its being, approaching humbly the shrine, renouncing that which impedes growth, accepting the spiritual laws as those which govern progress. The will giveth rebellion. To castigate thy servant maketh an obedient member. Thus must discipline be established, control made manifest. The will lendeth itself to control, the flame of Spirit fanning the urge which, dormant, forceful, demandeth subservience. The Cross, thy symbol, shall adorn thy consciousness, for therein lieth all thou art. To purify must thou instill this, the symbol of the crucifixion, therein. It formeth the eternal, the all-enduring, symbol through which soul maketh the ascent. Allegorical, the unthinking mind seeth this, the symbol of the Divine. He who knoweth not love knoweth not its significance. Thus Jesus bestowed that which shall adorn the soul, the consciousness, of the believer throughout the eternal ages. It exemplifieth the supreme achievement, the ascent to that which initiateship delineateth. A disciple thou art when thou hast made of soul a Temple dedicated to the service of the Supreme Will. Thus doth the disciple become manifest, service being the key which openeth the portals of the Divine.

Oracle Fifty-Nine

He who speaketh ill of his brother denoteth a weakness within the self. He seeth the reflection of that which he hath not conquered. He glimpseth not the radiance of the Divine, the illuminating spark which denoteth the tie of brotherhood. He seeth not the path which lieth in advance, through which soul must in suffering come into the understanding the Supreme Will demandeth. Canst thou vision the weakness of thy brother with compassion, with the desire for alleviation? The mirror of thy weakness lieth revealed when thou castest the cold stone of censure, of adverse comment. Beloved, concentrate thou upon the Divine within each soul. Thus art thou disarming him who would harm thee. Thou too wert weak, else thou couldst not glimpse the Light. For, ever the dusk of the darkened night giveth way to the dawn. Thus the mind respondeth to the impetus of Spirit's urge by imperceptible degrees. The twilight of thy adolescence hath faded into the shadow of the Unseen, rebirth dimming the memory of that which was. Thou seest but the present. Thou art thus shielded, that soul through the turning backward of memory's leaves dwell not on that which was. Thus would growth be deterred. Thou seest but the present in which thou art. Therefore glimpse thou within each soul that which it must in the ultimate become. Thus is thy understanding made manifest. The past from which thou didst evolve lieth revealed within the Eternal Records. When thou selfless art thou mayest scan this, the thread of thy experience. For, in thy seamless robe, thou too shalt serve humanity beneath the Christic principle even as thy Brother in selfless being serveth thee. The heaven to which thou aspirest lieth in thy understanding, the plane of consciousness in which thou art merged within the Universal Mind, which exemplifieth the Supreme Will. There lieth the haven of the soul, the retreat which formeth the ultimate of desire. He who seeketh a haven wherein soul reposeth, with naught of effort for service, buildeth a mirage. For within service lieth the Father's will. The Nirvana of suspended effort is but the mirror of the mind, reflecting to thee thy desire, which, selfish, denieth to thy brother the aid which He, from celestial being, extendeth unto thee. Thus soul serveth soul, this being the Law irrevocable, supreme.

He who with blinded vision seeth not the spiritual essence of being denoteth a stage of evolution wherein Spirit's flame lieth dormant. It reposeth within the soul structure, through its dim radiance impelling action, but within the impetus is that which is as the shadow of its strength when to soul cometh the awareness of the Divine. Soul is as a captive bound by the chain of adolescence, which restricts the vision, limiting it to that which the understanding embraceth. Based on the material desire, soul motivateth in the groove of indulgence through which it, with an increasing fervor, reacheth out for the gratification of the senses. Soul, being the means through which thought findeth expression, determines the course by which experience taketh place, the broad field of exploration giving access to entrance according to soul's innate and predominating need. Soul through free choice entereth therein, in diversified measure drinking from the goblet provided with which to quench its thirst. It maketh choice impelled by the ever-present Guiding Force, which, cognizant of its need, indicateth through the concentrative ability the exact field of activity applicable to growth. An intricate process this through which soul unfoldeth, trending the path evolution provides from incipient being to the selfless status.

Oracle Sixty

Beloved, thy Elder Brother speaketh. He would that thou shouldst pay heed to His words. Thou who with blinded vision turnest from the spiritual universe, centering thy yearning on the indulgence of desire—what hast thou with which to enrich the consciousness? When transition taketh place and thou discardest the physical garment, functioning in the spiritual analysis, with what wilt thou embellish thought? Thus soul expresseth, extracting from the consciousness that which it hath embedded therein. This denoteth the treasure of the mind, that which thou hast garnered, traversing the broad thoroughfare of physical endeavor. Thou canst retain but the pure essence, casting aside the waste of selfish purpose. Meditate on these, my words. Within thy consciousness lieth all thou art. There repose the seeds of past endeavor. Hast thou stored therein that which shall support thee when thou ascendest to, in retrospection, weigh on the scales of divine comprehension its content? If thy store be depleted, barren as the desert shall be the expression of thy mind. For, within the realm of spiritual interpretation man retaineth but the gold of constructive measure. Within these words lieth a problem of profound significance. The babe prattles in its infancy, delineating its immaturity. The adolescence of childhood denoteth the birth of thought; the power to reason becometh apparent. The mature state giveth to man the ability to, in constructive measure, build that which is of superlative value. Art thou demonstrating this, the rare gift of reason? Or art thou through dalliance, through procrastination, wasting these, the fleeting hours? When the call cometh wilt thou joyfully respond? Or wilt thou strive to halt the Grim Reaper who giveth to thee the summons? Man knoweth not the hour the flame of physical being is dimmed to extinction. To, in faith, build with each passing moment the structure of the soul, reinforcing it with the pure cement of constructive effort; to embellish the Temple of Thought with the jewels of compassion—this giveth to thee that which imperishable is. When thou passest through the portals of the Infinite thou art as one of countless souls who have preceded thee. According to the soul-structure, its inherent strength, doth soul ascend to, in a comprehensive analysis, scrutinize that which it hath builded. It seeth the perfected masonry or it vieweth the faulty foundation which through a successive existence must be painstakingly reconstructed. It maketh the advance or it, through the retrogressive tendency, descendeth to the plane of its predominating desire. No soul maketh ascent above its inherent desire. Couldst thou rise above the yearning which lieth within thy soul, motivating action? If thou centerest thy yearning on the indulgence of the senses thou must of necessity function on a plane of like measure, there to in satiation view the effect which lieth within the cause. If thy soul yearneth for constructive effort thou art a builder, to, in unison with other souls of like status, create that which through its purity shall endure. Through segregation thou seest the result of evil. Through unity thou knowest the joy of constructive yearning. The law of preordination forceth each soul to the exact plane it hath earned in the existence but completed. He who with clear vision glimpseth in Nature the divine handiwork hath, within the Temple of the soul, permitted entrance of the Holy Light. It illumineth, with an increasing radiance permeating thought, giving expression through that which the creative instinct supplieth. That which hath the divine imprint alone surviveth. All else

fadeth as the flower, its petals, shriveled, blown into the
nothingness of space by the harsh wind of Time. Thus
the material mind createth, be it of art, of the strain
of melody, the canvas which through its irrelevant tone
beareth not the holy essence of creative instinct. That
which endureth hath within its composition the imprint
the Guiding Force bestoweth. For He who superviseth
thy physical endeavor hath through selflessness made
the ascent to the Christic consciousness. Thus He vieweth thy weakness, thy faltering effort, with the divine
comprehension His understanding bestows. Nature,
through which the Supreme Will is expressed, giveth
to thee a panorama of superlative beauty. Immerse thy
soul in the grandeur, the magnitude of her infinitude.
Thus art thou communing with the forces of the Divine.
Thou seest not the cosmic essence which permeateth
each leaf, each infinitesimal creature which findeth
being in her mighty kingdom. Thou seest but the outward manifestation of the Father's will, His supreme
handiwork. If thou wouldst with clear vision enter this,
the Temple of the Divine, thou wouldst attune thy ear
to the inner harmony which motivateth the universe.
Thy soul in response would vibrate to this, the celestial
symphony. The unbeliever denieth that which the physical vision embraceth not. The scoffer repudiateth that
which the physical ear hath not the ability to record.
Whyfore deniest thou that of which thou art a part?
The cosmic essence which sustaineth thee, which motivateth thy pulse, findeth its source in this, the invisible,
the intangible, universe. There lieth the source of all
thou art, the physical organism but delineating a brief
phase of thy soul's unfoldment. If thou wouldst through
comprehension penetrate this, the mystery of thy being,
thou must with profound humility approach the shrine

of Universal Being, seeking through thy faith to penetrate its mystery. Faith alone giveth unto thee entrance
to the realm of divine interpretation. And there lieth
the motivating power through which taketh place the
creation of the individual soul.

Oracle Sixty-One

He who maketh the ascent to the immortal status hath completed the evolutionary cycle. His soul hath through unfoldment emerged from the infancy of thought, progressing through innumerable existences to the attainment of the mature, the intellectual, status. Thus soul maketh the ascent, immortality being the ultimate of all. Here commenceth the ascent through which the Christic consciousness becometh the supreme achievement. Soul passeth through the varying planes of consciousness demonstrating its strength, its worthiness for an advance. It through the creative instinct perpetuates its being. For within this lieth the source of all that is. Each soul createth according to its innate strength, on whatsoever plane of consciousness it functions. Thus cometh into being the divine melody whose haunting loveliness charms, which liveth eternally in the realms of interpretative thought. Bestowed through the concentrative ability within the consciousness of one attuned through the yearning for unfoldment (conscious or subconscious, as it may be), it becometh apparent as an actuality. *Inspiration,* man termeth this, the transposing of the Divine. Each soul in immortal being thus createth, making the ascent, each advance denoting the accentuation of the spiritual cadence which permeateth the creative instinct. Alternating the activity of creative bliss with the service which formeth equal part of soul's activity, soul progresseth until through the innate selflessness it becometh a servitor of the Master Jesus, to, in service to humanity, exemplify the Christic instinct.

Service it is which giveth to soul the ability to make the advance, service on whatsoever plane of consciousness it functions, through the compassionate instinct alleviating the need. He who serves, who striveth to lift from another the burden, exemplifieth the Divine Will. He who knoweth not the yearning to alleviate hath not come into an awareness of the purpose of his being. To glimpse the suffering of humanity with the calloused vision is to dwell within the darkness of the mind. Mind it is which imposeth a hardship on soul. It through habit thrusteth upon soul the desire of ulterior motive. Mind, through which soul expresses, serveth twofold. It accepteth the dictum of soul, giving obedience thereto. Or it as an independent agent extracteth from the consciousness that which it hath recorded of adverse effort, in activity striving to delineate desire. Mind through its facile adaptability maketh a servant of supreme value. Or it through disobedience causeth that for which soul must in an additional existence make amends. To, in thought-control, subjugate the mind is to, in constructive effort, build that which endureth.

Oracle Sixty-Two

Soul, beset by desire, committeth adultery. Herein lieth an offence against Nature, which through the propagative instinct furthers creation. Man, impelled by desire, through the gratification of the senses doeth that which weakens the morale, which teareth apart the resistance. Desire it is which thrusts upon soul the urge for satisfaction. To deny desire through the process of thought-control is to reinforce the strength of will. He who committeth in thought the act which desire inflicts hath in offence to Nature perpetrated disobedience. He hath builded the thought-form of the reality. Within the consciousness lieth embedded the image of the act, there to remain until, through the comprehensive analysis which transition fosters, it is scrutinized with the understanding of its import. Adultery is the sharing with another in companionate union the fruits of passion. Herein lieth the means of propagation. Frustrated, it worketh on soul an injury. It is the abuse of the law of creative impulse. The loss of virtue, man calleth this, the indulgence of the senses without the boundary the marital status imposeth. The physical law interprets this as an offence through which the dissolution of the marital tie is warranted, with a corresponding humiliation as the issue. The spiritual law taketh cognizance of the desire which in thought perpetrated the offence. Knowest thou the reason for this differentiation? He who judgeth another's weakness through the dense fog of material vision seeth but the physical implements employed. He giveth decision according to the law through which control is demonstrated. Jesus in allegorical delineation lifted the Magdalene, healing with the tender compassion manifest. Who existeth in physical form who hath not sinned in thought? Who hath not experienced the pangs of jealousy, of hatred, of adverse and censorious regard? Who liveth who can in uprightness stand forth as an ideal of purity? To censure, to condemn another in bitter reprisal, denoteth a profound weakness. Thou who walk in physical being knowest diversified weakness. If thou wert pure, holy, thou wouldst in immortal accord serve thy Elder Brother. Therefore be thou lenient in thy judgment, healing with thy tender compassion. Censure not the Magdalene nor him who partaketh jointly. Know that the Guiding Force giveth to each soul the temptation necessary for experience, the temptation which soul must reject, demonstrating its innate strength, or before which it must fall, to through remorse, with a comprehension of error, glimpse its predominating weakness. Time, the gaunt disciplinarian, bringeth to each individual soul the realization of its own deficiency. Thou who serve the Master shall through thy example teach thy erring brother the futility of indulgence. To condemn weakeneth thine own resistance to defeat. To glimpse with compassion another's weakness is to exemplify the understanding which is the ultimate of all.

Beloved, wouldst thou receive the wealth of the physical universe? Or wouldst thou from choice possess the treasure of the mind? Wouldst thou in golden shekels dwarf thy soul? Or wouldst thou in thought, permeated by the spiritual essence, reflect the Divine? The choice lieth within thee. If thou centerest thy yearning on the material, which perishes, which withstandeth not the harsh wind of adversity, thou hast builded the replica of thy desire. That which thou buildest in thought, in profound concentration interjecting thy yearning, thou hast created. It shall in the existence yet to come give unto thee thy desire. It shall automatically, when transition taketh place, transpose thee to the plane where dwell these, the builders of material aspiration. There wilt thou further thy longing, interspersed with the necessity for analysis of this, the inner yearning of thy soul. Shouldst thou rise above this, the material, thou makest an advance. If tenaciously thou clingest thou wilt descend to, in physical experience, test thy strength. Therefore scrutinize with far-vision the motive involved. For what purpose desirest thou that which perishable is? If thy desire indicateth thou hast discarded material aspiration, glimpsing within the golden sheen the tarnished thread, thou art immeasurably enriched. For, ever as the sun gleaming in the dome of Nature's infinitude illumineth for thee thy day, so shall its spiritual replica, which is the love-force emanating from the Supreme Power which motivateth the universe, illumine thy soul, that its radiance blind thee not to the need of mankind. Thus thou choosest that which enricheth or that which depleteth the content of thy soul.

Oracle Sixty-Three

If one came unto thee in robe of gleaming white, speaking words of wisdom, if thy physical vision embraceth not the celestial visitor but thy spiritual perception revealeth this, the Holy Presence, wouldst thou make denial or wouldst thou with the soul give joyous greeting? Such a visitation taketh place when soul through the subservience of the will maketh the ascent to the plane of the Divine. It receiveth the Holy Audience, to in homage, in humility, prostrate the self. It, immeasurably enriched, descendeth to through the physical organism reveal the radiance it hath attained. Thus soul, enriched, receiveth that which strengthens, which giveth incentive for renewed growth. He who maketh the ascent holdeth sacred to himself this, the celestial visitation. He, in the sanctuary of the soul, guardeth the conscious knowledge of the privilege bestowed. When the material mind turneth to the source of its being, accepting the spiritual interpretation, it casteth aside its prejudice, which is as a glacier repelling with frigid antagonism the one whose understanding hath given entrance to the Holy Audience. Ever doth antagonism enwrap ignorance, wearing as a robe the adolescence of restricted thought. He who permitteth his soul to experience this, the shaft of hatred, layeth bare the wound which hath been healed. Thou canst not implant thy seed within the uncultivated soil, demanding the fruitful harvest. The seeds of divinity likewise perish when thou hast striven to impregnate the barren soil. Thou canst nurture with the compassion which prepareth the soil, leaving to the Guiding Force the implantation when through growth soul receptive is. I would thou shouldst through understanding of these, the spiritual laws, govern thy course. Give generously, lavishly, of thy love, mingled with pity, when thou sensest the need. Protect thine own soul from injury, lest it incapacitate thee, bruising thy faith.

Oracle Sixty-Four

He whom thou knowest as Jesus, who hath through the crucifixion ascended the Cross, giving to humanity the supreme pattern on which to build the soul-structure, speaketh through the Living Word. He giveth that through which shall humanity take cognizance of His living presence. He speaketh thus that the unrest, the prevailing anguish, be mitigated; that the order of Brotherhood become established. For only thus, through the recognition of the tie which uniteth soul to soul, shall man conquer the spirit of greed which permeateth the mass-thought. Only thus shall avarice become non-existent, shall love unfurl the emblem of eternal and universal significance, to beneath a common leadership guide humanity from the dangerous course of indulgence which leadeth to destruction. Humanity through blinded vision glimpseth but the mirage of its own desire. It pursueth the path of indulgence. It seeth not that naught lieth therein but the bitterness of defeat. The Master, through the medium of thought, speaketh that humanity take heed. He who turneth away, refuting the call, suffereth a loss. He who heedeth, his soul responding in recognition of the Voice, receiveth the Light which in illumination shall outline for him the path. Love is manifest, that love which, depthless, embraceth with the essence of divinity. Ever, when necessity demandeth, doth the Living Presence become manifest. He who speaketh cometh to, through the Word, reveal the survival of the soul, the ageless, eternal promise exemplified through the Living Thought. Through thought soul communeth. It is the eternal expression of divine interpretation. From the heights cometh the Voice, pleading that humanity take heed of this, the call; that it turn to that which alone giveth peace; that it shorten the period of anguish, lifting soul to the plane from which it vieweth the futility of error, of procrastination. The Holy Presence in benediction placeth upon this the seal of authentic communion, which delineates the means through which humanity receiveth the Word, within which lieth the Law. Selah.

Oracle Sixty-Five

Thou, who art of the physical universe: listen to the words of the Master who speaketh unto thee. Compassionate the instinct which prompts, motivated by that love which, depthless, probes the need of humanity. Whyfore art thou weary, oppressed? Thou hast turned from the pure, the holy, centering thy yearning on that which endureth not; which, born of desire, perishes as the flower. Thou hast pursued the phantom of illusion, believing that therein lieth the panacea for thy woe. If thou wouldst rend the veil which obscureth thy vision thou must in a humility which is depthless approach the shrine of thy yearning, there to immerse thy soul in the healing waters. Thus alone is absolution bestowed. Man wearieth of the baubles of the mind; as a weight they impinge upon the consciousness. Embedded within this, thy record, lieth all thou art. Each thought, imprinted with pristine clarity, revealeth thy stage of unfoldment. If thou couldst with clear vision scan this, thy soul's achievement, thou wouldst turn from the darkness, seeking within the Light for that which alone satisfieth. Unto thee cometh the Beloved Healer, who ministereth to thee. Canst thou not accept that which He giveth? He seeth thy need, thy hunger. For within thy unrest is all revealed. He glimpseth the weakness which desire imposeth, which as a scourge forceth thee to adverse effort. In the distance thou glimpsest the rainbow, which lures thee. If thou couldst immerse thy soul in this, the radiant aura of Nature, thou wouldst weary of its purity. For thy soul reacheth for that with which it may satisfy desire. Thy desire centereth not on the pure, the holy. It yearns for that which debaseth. If thou couldst reach the star thou wouldst with it adorn thy yearning, glimpsing not its significance but seeking in selfish purpose to wear as a bauble that with which to create envy in thy associates. Perverse thy effort, for within it lieth not that which uplifteth, sustaineth, but that which teareth apart the morale, inflicting the hardship of despair. He who in indulgence gratifieth the self buildeth that which in anguish of soul he must demolish. Each stone shall be as a monstrous weight which must in comprehension be lifted from the consciousness. Canst thou not see the folly of error? The Light which illumineth for thee the path revealing is. It showeth thee the way. It giveth unto thee the laws which govern soul's endeavor; that which in the ultimate soul achieves. He who listeneth, taking heed of these, the words of the Master, shall in understanding make the advance; shall shorten immeasurably the evolutionary cycle which thou must complete ere to thee is given entrance to the realm which immortal is.

Oracle Sixty-Six

Thrice have I come unto thee and thrice hast thou
denied Me. Through the Living Thought which pierceth thy consciousness cometh the Voice. Thou, who
turnest from the path of selfish endeavor; who, heeding
the call, givest response—it is to thee thy Elder Brother
speaketh. Thy Light it is which shall illumine for thy
brother the path. Upon thee lieth the responsibility of
example. For thus shalt thou draw to thee the weaker
member. A staff thou art upon which the weak, the halt,
shall lean. For within the radiance of thy aura shall
strength be found for like measure. Therefore guard
well that which is thine: the Light which thou hast
visioned, which illumineth thy soul, reflecting the divine
radiance. What maketh a Light?—thou askest. The
Light cometh from within. It is the Spirit, which is the
incipient and divine element of thy being; the ageless,
eternal emblem of the Father's creation. For thus alone
He in His infinite and supreme wisdom createth the
individual soul. Thou who art in darkness—thy Light
shineth not. For thou hast denied the source of thy
inception. Until thou turnest in humility, in subjugation
of thy will, thou canst not reflect the Light eternal. For
within darkness existeth not the Light but within the
Light doth darkness become as naught. Thou speakest
of Light, comprehending not its significance. Thou seest
the material manifestation which is as the shadow of
the real. Naught which exists in tangible form revealeth
reality. For within the shadow lieth not the substance
but within the substance lieth all that is. Therefore the
etheric, the spiritual, universe delineateth that which
endureth, which thy Elder Brother termeth reality. Man
findeth not in a dream the substance. He glimpseth but
the shadow. The physical universe within which thou

undergoest the varying phases experience provideth is but a fragment of thy soul's activity. The material mind seeth in the physical manifestation all that is. Thou canst not thus interpret the soul's endeavor. Thou glimpsest but that which thy near-horizon revealeth, but thou deniest not that which lieth afar. Therefore why deniest thou that of which thy physical senses taketh not cognizance? Thou seest the dome of Nature's infinitude which is the far-horizon of thy physical vision. Couldst thou pierce this, the infinitude of space, revealed unto thee would be the universal principle, which composeth all that is. Thou glimpsest the sun whose radiance giveth unto thee thy sustenance but thou seest not its dimension. Nay, Beloved, the physical vision embraceth not its true significance. For thou, with the physical vision, canst not pierce this, the mystery of creative being. Thy perception alone giveth to thee the power of interpenetration of space. Thou who in physical being function hast not this, the power of immortal status. Revealed unto thee is but an infinitesimal part of that which thou art. When thou canst in comprehension of thy frailty accept the divine interpretation of thy being, when in humility, depthless, immeasurable, thou canst approach the sanctuary of the Divine, then thou shalt enter into the comprehension which giveth to thee the key which openeth for thee the portals of thy understanding.

Oracle Sixty-Seven

What maketh of Living Thought a reality? Thought, through which soul giveth expression, delineates the process of communion. It is thus soul communeth with soul, receptivity being the necessary attribute. Purity maketh of soul an instrument. It giveth the receptivity through which it casteth aside prejudice, condemnation. It hath renounced selfish desire. The will subservient is to the Divine. It imposeth naught of selfish purpose. Thus soul becometh receptive to the divine inflow of thought. Such a process denoteth the means through which inter-communion becometh an actuality. Thus the Living Thought floweth forth through the channel of instrumentation, that humanity receive these, the laws of universal import. He who accepteth, dwelling within their tenets, hath in renunciation crucified desire. He who refuseth, who scoffeth, turning from the Light, entereth into the darkness of disbelief wherein the Light penetrateth not. Experience alone bringeth to this soul that which dissolveth the barrier soul hath erected between the self and the Divine. Time through experience administers the salt of tears which, through disillusionment, teacheth soul the source of its strength, which revealeth in clarity the depths of its weakness. Thou too wert weak, Beloved, else thou couldst not have come into that through which thou acceptest the words of the Master. Therefore permit thy compassion, which is the healing essence of love, to flow forth to enfold thy weaker, thy erring, brother.

Oracle Sixty-Eight

He who holdeth a harsh thought against his brother
buildeth that which shall recoil against the self.
Thought, a powerful factor, reacheth the object of its
concentration, with subconscious awareness. Therefore
discipline thy mind, that it reflect but the essence of
compassionate regard. He who through selfish purpose
inflicteth a hardship on a companionate soul buildeth
that through which shall the karmic principle, operative, reveal through trial and tribulation the extent of
the error involved. Therefore, Beloved, thou art cau-
tioned: exemplify love, whose root is understanding
tinged with compassion. Soul through weakness delineateth a selfish motive. Greed, which is a near kin, domi-
nates thought. For he who selfish is thinketh not of
another. He liveth for the self. Couldst thou with a clear
vision glimpse the soul thus afflicted thou wouldst with
pity enwrap. Long and devious the course soul must
traverse ere to it cometh an awareness of its inherent
and predominating weakness. Selfishness denoteth a
profound weakness in the morale. It reflecteth that
which makes of soul a harsh task-master. He who liveth
for the self taketh not heed of another's suffering. He
turneth an ear deaf to the need of humanity. His soul
vibrates not to the love-current which through its potent
essence maketh for understanding. The Law which
worketh irrevocably, unremittingly, giveth to each that
which fosters growth. As the pendulum it swingeth to the
limital point before a reversal taketh place. Twofold
the law of karmic delineation, bestowing the dregs of
bitterness, or the tincture of bliss.

Oracle Sixty-Nine

The Voice speaketh, vibrant with tenderness. It calleth, giving to the individual soul the promise of a compensating peace. It outlines the path which leadeth to the Light, which eternal is. Canst thou refuse this, the Voice of the Master? Thy soul giveth response if thou wilt but renounce selfish purpose, turning from that to which thy adverse yearning leadeth thee. Thou art renouncing but that which bodeth ill, that which worketh harm. Dark the mind which permitteth not entrance to the Light of love, which filters through illumining when the sealed portals of antagonistic regard swing wide, revealing soul as a tabernacle dedicated to the Master's service. Soul erecteth an altar before whose holy radiance it lighteth the taper of pure intent. Thus soul giveth response when the love which floweth forth entereth. As the dawn it cometh, the shadows of the night giving release to the beatific Light. Thus soul becometh illumined, the transformation becoming apparent through the quickening of the understanding, which permeateth thought. Couldst thou vision the Temple of the Infinite thy soul through response would vibrate to its holy radiance. Build thou within thy soul a Temple whose portals admit the entrance of love, which is the all-pervading essence of the Divine. Bar not the Angelic Host, for thus art thou sustained through thy invisible Brothers who, in selfless being, attend thee. No soul exists who traverseth the path of experience in solitary state. By the comparative issue is growth fostered, initiative bestowed. No soul in physical being chooseth the channel of exploitation. For the Guiding Force, which superviseth, holdeth before the object of its concentration the mirror of desire in which is reflected the image of its inherent yearning. He who attendeth thee, through the understanding which is depthless, immeasurable, knoweth thy innate need. He seeth the predominating weakness: greed, selfishness, pride, the yearning for worldly acquisition. He, with the far-vision the selfless status bestows, giveth to thee that through which experience, with the ever-attendant disillusionment, accompanied by satiation, shall purge thy soul of its predominating weakness. Therefore, Beloved, take heed of these, the words of the Master. Beneath the All-Seeing Eye each soul functions, the motive of each act scrutinized and weighed upon the scales of unprejudiced and supreme judgment. Thus serve the invisible Brothers of Humanity who in selfless being demonstrate the supreme and omnipotent will, Jehovah.

Oracle Seventy

Beloved, I would that thou shouldst scrutinize thy every thought; analyze its content, separating from the pure the impure, from the uplifting the degrading, from the constructive the destructive. Only thus mayest thou determine through control the outward expression of thy soul. Thy thought it is which giveth birth to the act, to the spoken word, by which thou art known. He who speaketh in words of wisdom giveth that which is as a beacon of light, which showeth the way, which delineates that of which the weaker member is uncomprehending. He who through deficient control prattles idly denoteth a lack of content within the consciousness which Time, the invisible task-master, with the tools of experience shall correct. He who debaucheth the mass-mind with the impurity which is innate, inherent, giveth that which through its ill odor is as a decadent weed, whose demise offendeth the nostrils. Thus the impure contaminates the pure. The weed groweth within the garden of the mind, communicating to other minds its inherent tendency. Seest thou the necessity for the control of thy soul's expression. Thou knowest not to what extent thou hast impregnated thy neighbor's garden with thy adverse content. Transition alone, with its corresponding comprehension of error, will reveal to thee the extent of thy wrong-doing. He who implanteth within the mind of another an adverse yearning buildeth a debt which must be obviated. The thorn of hatred shall fester, becoming through its contagious quality a monstrous wound. Thus grow the adverse weeds of thought, which find their incipient being through thwarted desire, through envy, fostered by selfish instinct. Revealed to thee in their pristine nakedness are these, the weaknesses to which thou art subject.

Oracle Seventy-One

He who traverseth the byways of experience, holding close his garments that they brush not the weak, the halt, the lame, denoteth a pride which forebodeth disaster. He who refuseth to bind the wound, to, with the tender compassion of love, heal the bruisèd soul, denoteth a harsh and undisciplined nature. Pity is non-existent. He giveth not of the alms of sympathy, of understanding. Jesus, thy Elder Brother, through His ministrations to humanity differentiated not. Freely He bestowed; impartial the solace. Canst thou not do likewise? If thou acceptest these, the teachings of the Master, how canst thou refuse to heed the plea of suffering humanity? The spiritual hunger demandeth appeasement. If thou, who hast, withhold from the needy soul the Bread of Life thine own store shall be depleted. For the Law readeth that he who giveth receiveth in like measure. He who taketh, giving naught, depleteth the content of his soul. Therefore take thou heed of these, the words of the Master. Share thou generously of that with which thy faith hath supplied thee. He who taketh for example the life of the Crucified One must in like measure exemplify His teaching. He must in a compassion depthless, sublime, enwrap the weaker member, who as a babe knoweth not the laws which govern the soul's unfoldment. He performeth the miracle of the sacred sacrament. He breaketh the Bread of Life. He shareth the wine of the spiritual essence. He partaketh of the Feast of the Covenant. All this he doeth when through love he manifests the Master's teaching. He kneeleth not before the altar of the secular structure. He prostrateth the self before the altar of the Supreme God, there receiving the manna which his own soul craveth, with which to supply his suffering brother. Man performeth the act. He drinketh from the goblet the fruit of the vineyard. He taketh the vow of eternal allegiance. He breaketh the bread the golden wheat provideth. Thinkest thou this consecration maketh of soul a pure and holy substance? These are but the outward manifestations of subservience to the Supreme Will. He who goeth forth among the weak, the suffering, who brusheth the brow upon which pain hath imprinted the Cross, who lifteth from the darkened mind the weight which crusheth with its intensity, who bindeth the wound the unbeliever hath inflicted—he it is who in the tabernacle of his own soul hath established communion with the Supreme Intelligence, performing the sacrament, the holy communion, which purifieth and strengthens, with a corresponding balm of peace. Beloved, take thou heed of these, the words of Jesus. Within thine own soul perform thou the holy sacrament. If thou canst approach the altar in filial devotion with these, thy brothers, in thy chosen tabernacle, realizing the significance of thy act, thou art in accord. But if thy lips drain the goblet and thou breakest the bread with aught of hatred, of condemnation, of adverse regard manifest, thou art in falsity entering the Holy of Holies.

Oracle Seventy-Two

Again the Living Thought poureth forth that to humanity be given the Word, which is the Law within which lieth the promise of eternal life. He who heedeth shall in corresponding measure enrich the consciousness. He shall in comprehension of error turn from the false, the glittering brass which lureth, giving forth the shadow of the pure gold. He seeth with clear vision. He looketh through and beyond the physical existence. He seeth it as a vast plane on which countless souls struggle one with another, striving to wrest from experience the tithe which it provides. Knowest thou the reason for the descent into physical being? It is to test the mettle of thy soul structure. Thou knowest temptation. Passion lureth. Greed beckons, promising the acquisition of material appurtenance, of fame, of adulation. Thy pride sustaineth thee until through its insufficiency it giveth way and thou glimpsest it as a chain which bindeth thee. Thus shalt thou vision humanity when unto thee is restored the spiritual ability to comprehend human frailty. Thy perception it is through which thy vision is clarified. It is thus thou risest to the plane of a divine comprehension of the weakness which surroundeth thee. As a light flasheth is the call through which soul maketh known its yearning for the discarding of the fetters which bind. The light giveth evidence of its disillusionment, its desire for rehabilitation. The Guiding Force maketh response, sustaining soul, through concentration giving the incentive for effort. According to its innate yearning doth soul receive. Thus is growth fostered. The spiritual universe unfoldeth to thy perception by imperceptible degrees. The flower matureth thus, its petals unfolding to the warmth of the solar god. So thy Father solaceth thee, enwrapping thee with the love-force which bringeth to fruition the bud of thy spiritual understanding. Thou canst not blight the incipient bud unless another existence impregnate the soil of physical endeavor, to foster its growth. Thus the Supreme God, thy Father, enwrappeth thee with the holy essence of His love, that thy soul through unfoldment exemplify His power, which, omnipotent, giveth to thee all that thou art; which ordaineth that which thou shalt in the eons of the Infinite become.

Oracle Seventy-Three

Commandments have I laid upon thee, Beloved. Live thou within their tenets. Brotherhood demandeth the tie be strengthened. Cast from thee that which disturbs, which giveth to thee the profound unrest which permeates thy being. It lieth within thee, the divine element which prompts thee. With increasing intensity doth this, the divine spark, lend itself when through desire thy soul releaseth that which is as a barrier to growth. Each soul entereth into being created through the Supreme Will which omnipotent is. It unfoldeth according to the innate strength manifest. Thou canst through control increase this, thy soul's treasure. Or thou canst through excess, through indulgence, waste that which alone giveth to thee the elements of intrinsic worth. It lieth within the individual soul. He who receiveth the Word maketh unto that which his desire prompteth. He through grotesque imagery giveth form to the obscene, the mediocre; or, through the purity of his yearning, he createth that which beareth the divine imprint. Likewise thy soul respondeth to the Spirit's urge. If thou dimmest thy Light, through adverse effort forcing a fitful glow, an instability which sustaineth thee not in tranquil being, thou art employing the tools of mediocre, of adverse achievement. If thou, through control of thought, center thy yearning on the pure, the holy, thou art creating the imperishable masterpiece of divinity. The choice lieth within thee. Each soul buildeth according to the individual desire. Canst thou vision the ultimate? The path thou traversest leadeth where thy yearning indicates. It is of brief and narrow length or it through innumerable existences leadeth thee through the arid waste of inconsequential effort. When thou buildest with the tools of the Infinite thou art attuned to the realm of divine interpretation. By example thou givest to countless souls the pattern on which is constructed in like measure. Thus upon thee lieth the responsibility of choice. Wouldst thou through a faulty pattern give to thy brother that which in anguish of soul he must reconstruct? Or wouldst thou through the ideal presented lift to like effort the yearning exemplified?

Oracle Seventy-Four

Within the Law lieth the Word. Knowest thou the meaning of this, the irrevocable inscription of eternal consequence? The Law it is beneath which each existent soul functions. It outlines the breadth, the scope, of individual effort. None exceedeth its boundary. The Law it is which limits all existent life to a given groove or channel of activity. If thou function in harmony with the Law, accepting its dictum, and living within its tenets, thou art fulfilling thy destiny, that for which thou camest into being. If through denial thou frustrate that which sustaineth thee thou art in rebellion opposing the Source of thy being. The Law, irrevocable, supreme, is the active will of the Omnipotent God, thy Father, who ruleth the universe. All that existeth is the active creation of this, the Divine Will. The Law it is which ordaineth the operation of this, the all-abiding and eternal Will. If thou in love, in subservience, accept the covenants bestowed thou art fulfilling that which He hath ordained. Thou knowest the peace of a supreme content. Thou sensest the radiance of His holy presence. Thou art the free channel through which the love-current courseth, through which His will operative is. Thus thy Elder Brother delineates the Law. Within the Word lieth control. It is the Law operative, the individual, the systematic supervision which motivates the object, be it of whatsoever denomination. Carnate, discarnate, orb or creature—each existent atom functions through but one agency: the cosmic inter-penetration which alone sustaineth in active being. Thus the Word composeth the administering of the Law through the varying agencies which demonstrate control. The object functions through the Word which is the Law. What maketh the Word to operate? It is the Law, the Will omnipotent, supreme, of the Great Jehovah. Wouldst thou in puny effort defy this, the Supreme Will? When thou turnest from the Word, denying entrance to the love-force which alone sustaineth thee, when thou deniest Him who, through this, the Word, speaketh unto thee, thou art at variance with the Law. For, irrevocable, it compelleth each individual soul to, in the ultimate, accept its tenets; to bow the individual will to the Supreme. Thou but delayest the ultimate, forcing upon soul the necessity for additional experience through rebirth, with the accompanying pain and anguish. If thou wilt meditate upon these, the words of the Master, thou wilt find within them the cause which demonstrates the effect of thy unrest, thy weariness of soul, thy unavailing effort to find a surcease for thy pain. Man seeketh in physical means to allay his unrest. It lieth within the depths of thy soul, Beloved. Thou canst not find in the physical universe surcease for thy soul's craving. Thou canst bruise, canst tear to shreds the fibre of thy endurance, but the effect which causeth thy unrest still remaineth. The Great Physician, the Master Surgeon, alone through the depth of His compassion possesseth the power to alleviate that for which thy soul sickens and yearns. Canst thou differentiate between the stars which, in the infinitude of space, defy thy analysis? Doth thy vision embrace the varying degrees of distance which span their individual breadth? But one power alone giveth to thy soul the ability to thus probe the mystery of Nature's being. It is the power which the free, the selfless, soul exemplifieth when pure, holy, demonstrating the Christic consciousness. He, from the superlative heights, probes alike the heart of the universe, the heart of humanity, as it may be, visioning with the perception which penetrates the all, the need manifest. Thus speaketh the Master Surgeon that to humanity be given the awareness of His living presence. The Voice calleth to the individual soul, giving the promise of eternal peace to him who through renunciation casteth aside the selfish armour of prejudicial disbelief, which is as a barrier to understanding.

Oracle Seventy-Five

Thy Elder Brother giveth unto thee a stone. What lieth within its content? Crystallized, it repelleth entrance through physical means. Its surface giveth naught but resistance. Couldst thou with it sustain thy being, alleviating the hunger which consumeth thee? It is this which the prejudiced mind offereth to the inflow of the spiritual interpretation of being. It turneth the surface of a crystallized content. Harsh, antagonistic, it repelleth with egotistical self-sufficiency the manna through which its sustenance is assured. Man eateth from the loaf, denying its content. He taketh the Bread of Life which sustaineth, in denial refuting the taking thereof. If the love-force which, cosmic, permeateth the universe, sustaineth thee, the spiritual essence of divinity, how canst thou deny its existence? It permeateth each cell, each atom, of thy being. It causeth thy heart to beat, thy pulse to respond to the rhythm of Nature's harmony. Yet thou in denial refute its existence. Canst thou differentiate between the cell and the cell? Canst thou separate the thread of the fabric of thy soul? Canst thou pluck from the star its brilliancy, its radiance? When thou canst thus dissect the Divine, then in denial canst thou refute the existence of the spiritual universe, which encompasseth, sustaineth, thee; of which thou art a fragmental and atomic part. Thy mind defieth analysis. It supporteth thought, giving passage thereto. As a sieve it permitteth entrance within the consciousness. Thou canst not through analysis dissect its integral part. Beloved, the spiritual universe lieth within thee. It motivateth thy soul. Thus alone thou art. The Supreme Intelligence, thy Father, thus ordaineth. Each existent soul must in humility, in profound subjugation, bow to the irrevocable will of the Supreme Creator. There alone lieth the source of that which thou art. Thy Elder Brother through control exemplifieth this will; the Mediator, He who in universal control maketh operative the Supreme Will, in profound humility bowing thereto. Canst thou not likewise serve the Father whose love, depthless, measureless, enfoldeth thee? He who giveth of his all receiveth in like portion. Thus readeth the Law within which lieth the Word.

Oracle Seventy-Six

The field of golden grain lieth before thee. Thou seest within its intrinsic seed the bread of life. Each grain representeth the whole of which it formeth an integral part. Thou seest the vineyard, the fruit rich in texture delighting thy vision. Each grape when in unity exemplifying its purpose filleth the cask. Thou seest the extent of the ocean's shore, each grain of sand dependent upon an atom of like measure for bulk. If thou wouldst in concentrative effort analyze these, the atoms through which Nature operates, thou wouldst unite the elements which provide the necessary attributes for physical being. The grain of sand standeth apart as the foundation upon which the physical structure resteth. The ripened grain provideth the sustenance through which the physical organism operateth. The vintage giveth to man that through which his thirst findeth appeasement. Herein lie the essentials of physical maintenance. What createth these, the implements through which man operates? Through the supervision of the vast Brotherhood who in selfless being serve the Master Jesus is provided this, Nature's bounty, which in lavish distribution supplieth sustenance. Symbolic these, the implements. Nature. which through the guise employed delineates the Supreme Will operative, defieth analysis through physical means. The brain serveth man as the instrument of mind, its ability dependent on the innate strength of soul, which, through expression in thought, utilizes its instrumentation. To subtract from the individual soul the cosmic essence which sustaineth, which motivates, would be to remove Spirit, the integral element. Cosmic this, the divine nucleus of soul's structure. Cosmic the force which floweth forth to, in universal distribution, sustain the universe. Therefore if man denieth that of which he formeth a part he refuteth the Source from which his being found derivation. The divine attribute formeth a part of each existent atom, the incipient part from which springeth being. The grain of sand, the fruit of the vintage, the bread of life, the individual soul— each separate atom formeth a fractional unit of cosmic delineation through which the Supreme Will operateth to, in universal manifestation foster that, which to the soul whose evolutionary cycle is incomplete, is veiled in mystery.

Oracle Seventy-Seven

Beloved, unto thee cometh the voice of the Master. He speaketh of that which man termeth Eternity. Glibly man prattles of that which giveth to soul release from the physical habitation. The immature soul thinketh transition affords the means of a suspended activity; that the heaven-world compriseth the haven of a profound and lasting bliss. Man entereth into a state of peace, of bliss, when through understanding of the spiritual laws he functions in harmony with the universal principle. Heaven lieth within the soul who through renunciation hath conquered selfish desire. The compensating peace provideth soul with the tranquillity of a profound content. Soul, attuned, experienceth the unity, the awareness of the Divine through which it cometh into its rightful heritage. *Heaven,* the material mind termeth this, the awareness of the spiritual universe. For if soul be not cognizant of the spiritual analysis it knoweth not peace. Therefore he who yearneth for the heaven of his seeking must through purification cleanse the consciousness; for, within the depths of the soul lieth the state of consciousness which man calleth heaven. The babe whose dormant intelligence betrayeth not the soul's status giveth evidence of a state of repose. It, through the unawareness of that which physical manifestation portends, calleth into being the protective measure. Innocence exemplified is, in the immature body. For the consciousness hath been veiled that memory, silenced, recall not the past experience through which evolution taketh place. The immature soul accepteth not the law of rebirth. It refuteth that which conflicts with the inherent desire, which urgeth soul to extract from the present existence the fullness of experience. To, in concentration, meditate on that which precedeth, likewise on that which lieth in advance, bestoweth a sense of insecurity, unrest. For the Spirit, active, thrusteth upon soul a subconscious awareness of the grave responsibility attendant. To each soul cometh the awakening, the consciousness of its responsibility when the evolutionary period hath reached the exact moment applicable to the procedure. The babe delineateth the innocence of the silenced, the dormant, mentality. The gradually increasing awareness of the object in close proximity is symbolic of the lengthier and prolonged process through which soul, traversing the cycle evolution demands, turneth with imperceptible finality toward the Light, of which a fractional unit formeth the nucleus of the soul.

Oracle Seventy-Eight

Beloved, whyfore have I come unto thee? That through the Word, which is the letter of the Law, thou mayest receive the call. Each soul, which in physical delineation functions, cometh into an awareness of the Divine when evolution provides the experience through which soul cometh into the comprehension of its innate and predominating weakness. If soul turn from the Light, refusing to heed the Voice which calleth, it cometh again into physical being to, through further experience, prepare the soil. For thus the garden of the soul may be likened. The seeds implanted symbolic are of the embryo grain which through cultivation rewardeth the custodian, bearing the fruitful harvest or revealing the empty tares. The soil of life impregnated is with the seeds of spiritual significance. If the soil denote a lack of receptivity the seeds of purity, of divine interpretation, perish. For the barren soil giveth forth insufficient nourishment to sustain, to nurture this, the divine impregnation. Thus soul respondeth. It accepteth, nourishing with a growing understanding of its import, or it through the closing of the mind casteth aside that which alone bestoweth the peace for which it seeketh. Naught of spiritual essence perishes in the sense of material delineation. The ever-present cosmic force which permeateth each object within the universe gathereth unto itself that which of it formeth a part. Realize that all that existeth cosmic is; that each leaf which groweth upon the tree vibrating is with this, the spiritual essence; that the pulse of the universe beateth in unison with the heart of man. All delineate the rhythmic beat of the etheric, the spiritual tempo which emanates from the source of the Supreme, the Almighty, God. In His sublime, His illimitable, wisdom He createth all that is, that it foster the elements of the Divine through which His will becometh manifest. I would that in thy soul thou shouldst erect a shrine, there in profound humility acknowledging the power, illimitable, immeasurable, of the Holy Presence. In filial devotion give unto Him thy soul's homage. For within His love, His beneficence, is all submerged. As in a mighty ocean, His love provideth the content for the individual soul which as a single drop formeth a part. Thy Father's love thus enfoldeth thee. His compassion, which is the foundation of the understanding, enwrappeth thee. It, through the awareness which encompasses all, knoweth thy inmost need and it giveth to thee that through which mayest thou enter the kingdom of the soul, within which lieth thy all in all.

Oracle Seventy-Nine

Thrice thy Elder Brother hath called thee. Tender the Voice, breathing of love, of compassion. He speaketh thus that thou mayest realize thy procrastination, thy dalliance. He calleth through the spoken Word, which representeth the Law. Thus the Word floweth forth to give unto thee the summons. Unto each generation in physical being cometh the call. The Voice speaketh and the soul respondeth or it refuseth according to its innate yearning. If experience hath, through the suffering inflicted, quickened the tempo of the spiritual pulse the beat respondeth to the harmonic rhythm, functioning in harmony therewith. The soul maketh response through the vibration to which it is attuned. All that exists maketh vibration in sustained measure. The leaf through its transparent delicacy giveth evidence of the cosmic force which permeates. The flower through its color-tone denoteth the vibratory measure. The orb through which man visions the physical universe revealeth its pigment through the vibratory essence Nature supplies. All that is vibrates to the cosmic element in varying degrees of progress. Thine own soul through cosmic affinity denoteth through its tempo the exact stage of evolution in which thou art functioning. Therefore cosmic is the universe and all that existeth therein. When unto thee cometh the Voice thy soul maketh response. Through harmonic affiliation it quickeneth the beat, lifting thee to an advance in consciousness. Or through lethargy it heedeth not, refusing the spiritual stimulus provided. It lieth within thyself, thy yearning manifest, the response. Thus again thy Elder Brother calleth. Wilt thou make response, casting from thee this, the lethargy of inactivity? Thrice hast thou received the call. Significant these words. Wouldst thou once again turn in

indifference, in refusal, from the beatific Light?
Wouldst thou through procrastination prolong thy
physical activities? The choice lieth within the individual soul. As the intonation of a silver bell cometh the
call. The Master speaketh. Beloved, cast from thee thy
inertia. Enter thou the vineyard of service. Thy Father
hath need of that which thou canst give. Dark and
sombre the veil which enwrappeth humanity. It por-
tendeth that of which suffering and anguish form the
major part. For thrice hast thou refusal given to the
summons. If thou wilt but cast aside the phantoms of the
darkness which beckon thee! False the promise. For
within selfish desire lieth but despair. It affordeth thee
but a momentary satisfaction. The material treasure
fadeth as a dream, for its substance builded is of that
which knoweth not continuity. Thy world, perishable,
denoteth change, insecurity. Thou knowest not that
which lieth in advance. Thy security lieth in thy soul's
achievement, which alone endureth, which giveth unto
thee the joy of rewarded effort. Phantoms of darkness
surround thee; astral the proclivity. Thou seest but the
physical manifestation. Thou seest not the surrounding
gloom of adverse thought which enwraps. For these
are the thwarted souls who, in the purifying process,
manifest their anguish through thwarted desire. Thou
canst disarm these, thy brothers, who in anguish refuse
the solace extended, if thou wilt in love build a barrier
which deflecteth. Thou canst disarm hatred with love.
Thou canst deflect antagonism with compassion. For
hatred pierceth not the shield love hath erected. It formeth an insurpassable barrier to adverse thought. He who
speaketh giveth alike to each soul the love through
which He heals. He enfoldeth each soul who through
yearning seeketh the solace of the healing inflow. Thou

canst in unison send forth in universal distribution that
which is thine. Love, which is the antidote, the panacea,
for pain, alone quelleth the troubled waters of humanity.
Beloved, the Voice speaketh unto thee. Come unto Me
all who in humility, in subjugation, would that the burden be lightened. Come unto Me and unto thee shall
be given that through which shalt thou vision the glory
of the Eternal Dawn.

Oracle Eighty

Subjugation is that through which the will submissive becometh. It in subservience giveth obedience to the Supreme Will, withholding naught. It maketh obeisance before the shrine of filial devotion, receiving the inflow of that which cleanseth, which lifteth, revealing the purpose of its being. Subjugation is the means through which soul maketh the advance, through which the spiritual perception becometh apparent. Man termeth this the withdrawing, the thinning, of the veil. The veil of which man speaketh is the barrier he hath erected through mind's insistence. For the spiritual universe enfoldeth, encompasseth, all that is. Man senseth not its presence because of the dense fog of disbelief with which he encompasses the self. He buildeth that which barreth entrance to the love-force, that which deflects the rays of the beatific Light. When through the insistence of Spirit he penetrates the armour of materialistic instinct which enwrappeth soul, he with the spiritual vision, which perceptive is, dimly glimpseth the shadow of the Divine. Soul maketh the ascent by imperceptible degrees. It cometh into the Light with blinded vision. For, glorious, radiant, soul must through growth, through strength, adaptable become to this, the spiritual force which permeateth the universe. When Sorrow knocketh at the portals of the heart it releaseth the restricting fetters which bind, making receptive that which through its adamant, its concrete, resistance deflecteth the holy ray. Thus Sorrow becometh an angelic guest who bringeth to soul glad tidings of an Eternal Day. When through understanding the mind, adaptable, thus receiveth the celestial visitor grief will be replaced with a deep and all-abiding joy. For the Beloved who hath answered the summons hath entered not into the darkness but hath entered into the Light of an advanced understanding. Thus Death masqueradeth that to man be bestowed the lesson of loss through which he seeketh the Divine.

Oracle Eighty-One

The Holy Word floweth forth that humanity take
cognizance of the Living Christ. Thus cometh the call.
He who would serve the Master Jesus must in unselfish
purpose heed the plea of suffering humanity. For thus
is exemplified the Law which in the Word becometh
manifest. Therefore heed thou the Word. Famine stalketh as a grim spectre. Disease taketh toll of human
cargo. The elements through adverse behavior give
proof of Nature's autocracy. Canst thou doubt that
within all lieth a purpose? Thinkest thou the unrest
manifest denoteth not a grave crisis in the massed souls
who function in physical being? Beloved, within all
lieth a purpose. To seek within the effect the cause revealeth unto thee the reason. For thy disobedience to the
spiritual law is apparent. Thou canst not in error perpetuate thy being. The Law demandeth that growth be
consistent. If thou turnest backward, seeking to retrace
in indulgence thy spiritual unfoldment, thou canst but
to a limital degree indulge thy lower nature. Thy senses
respond to the impetus of desire, which impelleth thee
to adverse measure. Canst thou not in comprehension
glimpse the ultimate? Ever doth the scales of divine
comprehension weigh thy effort. It swayeth to the degree
the Supreme Will demandeth when the reversal taketh
place, forcing soul to, in comprehension, face the result
of its inherent weakness, its indulgence, its procrastination. Thou hast transgressed the Law. In disobedience
thou hast refuted the guidance, divine in its concept,
which giveth unto thee the laws which govern thy spiritual activity. Thus the need of humanity becometh manifest. The Master speaketh through the channel of
instrumentation. He speaketh to humanity that it in response cast aside that which leadeth to despair. Imper-

sonal the means exemplified. Ever thus doth the Law demand. He who receiveth the Word knoweth but the joy of communion. Naught of selfish desire interfereth. Through renunciation the material plane becometh non-existent, soul functioning as Spirit that it through the channel of unimpeded effort receive the holy inflow. This denoteth that which man termeth *communion*. The unity with the realm of spiritual interpretation becometh an actuality. He who through renunciation hath crucified selfish desire, who hath the yearning to serve in whatsoever field the Divine Will indicateth, becometh an instrument which worketh for good. Thus the Master calleth that response be given; that the souls who in physical being function unite with These, the white-robed Brothers, in unison to serve the Master Jesus; that the current unrest be curbed; that the suffering be mitigated; that man in understanding work with and not against his brother. The Law readeth a Brotherhood of Man must be established. The spirit of greed must become non-existent. The halt, the lame, the suffering, through the compassionate instinct must receive alleviation. He who denieth but cometh again into physical being to, in acceptance, merge the refusal given.

Oracle Eighty-Two

As a shepherd thy Elder Brother attendeth thee. He calleth. He in compassion ministereth. He lifteth when He seeth the yearning manifest. He chideth that unto thee be given the laws of unfoldment. He cauterizeth when necessity demands, that the wound of thy perverseness be cleansed, made receptive to the healing process. All this He doeth that the Father's will be exemplified. He seeth in the individual soul the weakness manifest. His pity, His compassion, enwrap. He glimpseth the flickering Light of Spirit's flame. He seeth it dimmed to near-extinction or He seeth it glorified, its aura enhancing the soul's proximity. All this He seeth; tender the regard. Canst thou in love, in compassion, thus enfold thy erring brother? It is to this thou must achieve. Censure, condemnation, must become nonexistent. For he who compassionate is disarmeth hatred with love. The essence of his pity floweth forth as a healing balm. Unto thee cometh the Voice. It pleadeth that thou mayest sense the Living Presence. Canst thou refute these, the words of the Master? He who turneth away, denying the source, hath builded the barrier of his disbelief. For within these words ringeth the Holy Anthem, which through the eternal ages hath roused the soul of the penitent; which through their potent significance reveal the source of the inception. Thou canst not deny this, the Voice. For it ringeth within the depth of thy soul, revealing to thee thy innate need. It, through the spiritual profundity, revealeth the source from which thou receivest thine all. As spark to spark, this, the Voice, ringeth within thy consciousness, calling to activity memory, that it clarify thy vision. Even though thy lips denial give, thy soul acknowledgeth the source of this, the Word. Permit it to rouse thee, to lift thee from the

morass of thine own folly. Permit the Light to illumine
for thee the path of renunciation, the Light which, glorious, radiant, imperishable is. All else fadeth. As a breeze
bloweth, vanished is thy material treasure. The spiritual
alone sustaineth thee. Couldst thou with far-vision
glimpse that which through greed, selfishness, thou hast
builded thou wouldst in supplication turn. For within
subservience, in reversal, alone lieth that which shall
lift from thee the darkness which enfoldeth. Thou seest
a brief unrest, a temporary disturbance. Thy Elder
Brother seeth the debasement of the mass-mind which
through retrogressive instinct hath centered its yearning on the indulgence of desire. He seeth the arid waste
of frustrated purpose through which soul must pass to
reach the Valley of Peace, which alone provides the
manna which satisfieth the craving for alleviation. He
who payeth heed entereth the path which leadeth to the
heights. He maketh the ascent, casting from him as he
goeth the raiment of adverse desire. His robe becometh
with the ascent the radiant aura of the illumined soul.
Wouldst thou with the drab raiment of the unbeliever
enwrap thy consciousness? Or wouldst thou through
thy understanding enfold thy soul with the beatific
Light, which clarifieth for thee thy vision?

Oracle Eighty-Three

Ignorance provideth the garment with which the immature soul enwrappeth the self. Dense, opaque, it permitteth not entrance to enlightenment. It defieth penetration of the spiritual ray which illumineth. When thou seest one who thus exemplifieth the adolescent stage of evolution bruise not thine own soul through the futile attempt for enlightenment. Know thou that thy efforts unavailing are, that the Guiding Force alone seeth within the depth of the darkened mind. Evolution sheltereth the varying stages of consciousness. It provideth haven for each existent soul, be it on whatsoever plane of consciousness it functions. All grades must of necessity one to another provide comparative measure. How else is initiative fostered? If through segregation soul of like status function with its companionate member, with naught to provide example, wherein would lie the incentive for effort? Inequality provideth the means through which each soul, be it of whatsoever grade of evolution, maketh effort for the advance. The Law worketh in universal principle. Nature giveth evidence of the manifestation of the law of inequality. The universal kingdom produceth the varying grades of achievement. Thus the Law of divine ordination worketh, that in all manifestation of being, organic and inorganic, the incentive be fostered through comparative issue. Thus wealth giveth to man the means of distribution. Innumerable the grades provided for individual effort through the disbursement thereof, each grade affording the soul functioning therein the wherewithal for individual action. Thus soul to soul worketh the Law; the mature, the advanced, soul through achievement giving example whereby the immature soul profiteth.

Canst thou not see the responsibility which is thine—thou who hast glimpsed the Light? Exemplify that which through its uplifting quality giveth an ideal. Else that which thou hast builded shall crumble and fall, revealing the faulty masonry of its foundation. The law of inequality provideth for the physical universe the impetus for unfoldment. To, through the levelling of caste work in harmony one with another, exemplifying not hatred merged with rancour, but love which healeth—herein lieth the ultimate.

Oracle Eighty-Four

Thy Elder Brother speaketh in words of wisdom. Thou canst not penetrate the depth of their content unless thou seekest within thine own soul for enlightenment. The Spirit it is which illumineth for thee the Holy Thought, the Spirit which through its urge forceth soul to, in concentration, apply to the individual self the laws encompassed. He who peruseth, scanning but the surface, glimpseth but the shadow. He who in concentrative effort, impelled by the yearning for enlightenment, breaketh apart the enwrapping shell findeth within the kernel, the pearl of rarest value, that which he weaveth into a rosary of peace with which to adorn his consciousness. Thus the seeker receiveth according to his yearning. The words of the Master pierce the soul of him who receptive is, who drinketh the spiritual draught which as an elixir of balm quencheth his thirst. Man drinketh the wine which cometh from the fruit of the vineyard. It stupifieth his senses if he drinketh to excess. The Wine of Life thy Elder Brother calleth this, the divine vintage. For it is that through which Spirit, quickened, giveth to soul the halo of the Divine, the halo which through its radiance enhanceth thought, giving to it the rich content of profundity. The metaphor revealeth the symbology of the grape. Luscious, effervescent, within it lieth the tincture of the senses which quickeneth, exhilarateth, and destroyeth when in abuse its misuse becometh apparent. Nature giveth lavishly of her munificence. Man taketh, transposing that which beautiful is, in indulgence draining its content to his eventual harm. He maketh choice of free will. Within the cup lieth experience, which maketh of man a slave, the chains which bind revealing in the ultimate the deficient strength with which he striveth to break the fetters. Thus cometh disillusionment, satiated with despair. Excess maketh for pain.

Oracle Eighty-Five

Indulgence maketh of soul a slave. It bindeth. Cruel the means employed for bondage. When through bondage soul powerless is, the comprehension of freedom becometh apparent. Thus is incentive given birth for effort. He who hath not liberty sigheth for release. He through renunciation casteth aside the predominating weakness, rebuilding that which he hath destroyed. Error maketh of soul a weakened channel. Heir to physical disability, the flesh imposeth a multiplicity of ills. Thus is disease the direct result of error. Through indulgence the physical organism becometh receptive to that which error hath imposed. He who indulgence giveth to the senses, who through perversion gratifieth desire, hath within the body implanted the germ; for the abuse inflicted a transgression is against the law of Nature, which commandeth that each member involved receive but that for which its creation became apparent. The mind, through which thy soul expresseth, lendeth itself to adverse desire. It implanteth within the physical organism through the necessity for compliance, the response to muscular control; forcing upon the brain the dregs of its debauch. For within the brain lieth the means for compliance, it being the controlling agent of the nerve-centers which impel action. If thou abuse this, thy physical temple, thou workest a hardship on the morale, which dependent is on thy will-power, this being the stamina of thy spiritual structure. Canst thou not comprehend the intricate process involved? Thy soul, thy mind, thy consciousness—thy spiritual attributes—function through the physical to which thou apportionest the dregs of thy wasted effort. When in physical infirmity thou art submerged, the ill is that which thy excess hath builded. Perhaps within the thread of thy past experience lieth the weakness of thy present infirmity. Perchance within the existence yet to come wilt thou reap the harvest which in this existence thou art implanting within the soil of thy present endeavor. Thou canst not escape the consequence of thy adverse achievement. It lieth within thy consciousness, where thou hast implanted it, and only through thine own expatiation canst thou cleanse this, the consciousness, of the waste which thou hast stored therein.

Oracle Eighty-Six

He who harboreth a wrong buildeth that through which shall he a grievance experience. Within the consciousness he buildeth in thought-form the replica of that which he hath bestowed. Thought, through which soul giveth expression to desire, createth all that exists in physical form. For within the mind must of necessity be implanted the incipient seed before in actuality the object becometh manifest. Thought, which motivateth action, is in reality the source of initiative. It giveth to the mind the idea, which mind develops according to its innate strength, drawing from the consciousness that which it hath stored therein with which to adorn, to embellish the incipient idea. Therefore in thought-form must be created the replica before in tangible and physical delineation it taketh formation. If man harbor an enmity in retaliatory desire against his brother he buildeth the thought-form of the act of reprisal. He buildeth that which shall in return recoil upon the self. Seest thou the working of the Law? Irrevocable, it giveth to soul the exact portion it hath earned. When to man cometh the power to, through control, subject mind to obedience he hath become the master of the self. For Spirit through dominion forceth soul to reflect but the pure, the holy, desire. It knoweth naught of condemnation, for it seeth within each erring soul the ultimate when, selfless, it hath overcome the weakness which sappeth the strength as it giveth to desire full sway. When man smiteth thee turn not in reprisal thy effort but, calm, assured, heal with the essence of thy compassion, which is given birth through thy understanding.

Oracle Eighty-Seven

The bird wingeth its path through the infinitude. It goeth by instinct, which is the guidance which it receiveth through the ever-enwrapping folds of the mass-consciousness which protecteth creature existence. It seeketh by instinct the habitation through which it fulfilleth its destiny. Man seeth this, the exemplification of the Divine, with dim vision. For he looketh not to the source of its motivation. It goeth—it cometh—thus his mind maketh decision. Supervision giveth to the wingèd creature the power of instinct. It supplieth the sustenance through which it sustaineth being. It setteth man an example of intrinsic worth. He, who giveth to the creature the sustenance necessary for being, supplieth man with that which meeteth his innate need. Man sigheth for plenty. He demandeth surplus. He wasteth that which the Father createth for the common good. Waste entereth not into the divine plan. It is man who through greed demonstrateth this, the wasteful spirit. He ladeneth his table with the plenty which he taketh from the needy. He heareth not the cry of hunger, of want. Deaf, he pampereth the self. The Supreme Intelligence createth supply for every human need. If man through greed demonstrate monopoly he worketh that which causeth suffering, deprivation. He inflicteth a common cross which the needy of humanity must sustain. If the surplus benefit humanity through wise and judicious distribution he becometh a benefactor who demonstrates the working of the humane principle. What wouldst thou who possess a surplus of material acquisition? Wouldst thou in treasure imperishable enrich thy soul? Or wouldst thou in selfish indulgence impoverish the self? The choice is thine.

Oracle Eighty-Eight

If unto thee came one in the habiliment of poverty, beseeching aid, and thy table laden was with plenty, wouldst thou welcome thy brother, sharing with him thy feast? Or wouldst thou close against him the portal of thy dwelling? Jesus, the man, in physical manifestation drank from the cup of sorrow the dregs of anguish. He drained to completement the draught. Weary, He knew not the solace of that which luxury bestoweth. He walked among the poor, the lowly, in the spirit of brotherhood demonstrating His love. He shared with the disciples the crust. He gave unto the hungry the Bread of Life which imperishable is. If thou deniest thy brother that which sustaineth life within the frail habitation, then thou wilt hunger for the spiritual manna when thou through transition castest aside the flesh. For thou hast in denial refusal given to him who besought thee. Within thine own soul lieth the famine which comprehension, with a corresponding remorse, alone will alleviate. Thus worketh the Law.

Oracle Eighty-Nine

Unto thee have I spoken in parable, that thou mayest read within the Word the Law. If unto thyself thou takest these, the laws which govern soul's progress, thou shalt, immeasurably enriched, make the advance. If thou refuse, thou art as one who walketh with blinded vision, glimpsing not the danger which lieth before thee. Thy soul it is which supporteth thee; which through the mind, the body, expresseth desire. Within thy soul thy Spirit is; which, imperishable, divine, is that which thou art. Wouldst thou that it, through thy acceptance, increase its radiance, illumining the soul? Or wouldst thou that through refusal it dormant remain, permitting thee to, through folly, indulgence give to desire? Thy choice is that which maketh growth or that which bringeth thee into existence to once again trend the path experience provideth for the castigating of the baser self. Only thus art thou receptive, when through the comprehension of the weakness which is thine, thou in renunciation buildest anew the weakened fabric of thy soul. He who through acceptance giveth heed to these, the Master's words, becometh a power for good. He who refuseth but addeth to the adverse content which maketh of the mass-mind a deterrent force. Like to like, worketh the Law.

Oracle Ninety

A pool thy Elder Brother placeth before thee; stagnant the content. Naught refresheth the waters therein. Couldst thou dwell beside this, the dank manifestation, thou wouldst become as one bereft. Within this, the pool thou seest, thy Elder Brother droppeth the pure content, which as a miracle transformeth that which denoteth the adverse measure. He, by imperceptible degrees, transformeth. He maketh pure the impure. But of necessity must He deplete even as He replenisheth. Thus the mass-mind operateth. It denoteth the decadent content of a perverse desire. It, through its stagnant consistency, giveth forth that which offendeth the pure. Knowest thou the remedy? The tincture of pain, of unrest, of privation, He droppeth within this, the pool of human endeavor, that through the transmutation of the impure to the pure it change its content. Man seeth but the surface. The Master-Surgeon looketh within the depths, glimpsing the dregs which as a monstrous weight impede effort. Couldst thou thus probe within the individual consciousness thou wouldst perceive the necessity for a purification. Thou wouldst glimpse the dregs of greed, selfishness, envy, which thou hast fostered through indulgence. Unto thee is revealed the illness with which humanity is afflicted, that thou mayest glimpse within the current upheaval, the cataclysmic measure of Nature, the remedy applied.

Oracle Ninety-One

The beatific Light it is which illumineth thy soul. He who through its divine radiance motivates casteth aside hatred, rancour, prejudice, which giveth birth to retaliatory measure. For within the Light that which is, reflected is in pristine clarity; the weakness manifest, through which soul maketh the steep grade to initiateship, being revealed; the purpose lying therein. The Light eternal—man calleth this, the divine ray which in reality is the Father's love; His power supreme through which the universe and all therein motivateth. The atom which formeth through unity the cohesive element, impregnated by the cosmic inflow, exemplifieth the system, intricate, sublime, through which becometh an actuality the atomic principle. Man seeth but a minute portion of the means through which Nature functions, the mind through that which prejudice createth erecting a barrier which barreth from it the manifestation of the spiritual universe. Inseparable, intermerged, operate these, the dual manifestations of the Supreme Will, the spiritual replica being the initial design upon which the physical is patterned. Therefore if through prejudice man denieth the spiritual manifestation of being he automatically sealeth the portals of his understanding, refusal giving to the inflow of the interpretative and creative instinct. To separate the drop from the drop requireth intricate skill if through analysis its content be dissected. To, through the separative issue dissect the means through which Nature operative is, the skill of the believing, the enlightened soul, must be utilized. For only the soul whose faith sustaineth receptive is to the guidance through which the revelation, the unfolding of the mystery of creative being, taketh place. The unbeliever through prejudice barreth from his soul the Holy Light. For he dimmeth the Spirit's flame through which enlightenment taketh place. From within cometh this, the divine radiance, perpetuated by the cosmic inflow, which through its pristine and integral unit illumineth the soul through which it expresseth.

Oracle Ninety-Two

He who knoweth peace experienceth the bliss of the soul attuned. He hath in communion lifted soul to the realm where harmony motivateth and his soul's tempo beateth in unison therewith. The rhythmic cadence of the sublime sustaineth. Soul through unity hath established stability. It through receptivity to the Divine Guidance demonstrateth the faith apparent. Thus the physical universe ceaseth to fret, to torment, with the varying experiences through which it hath conquered desire. The soul hath renounced selfish purpose, the innate yearning being for enlightenment, for unfoldment. When to soul cometh the realization of the perishability of that which material is it ceaseth to, in a spirit of greed, of acquisitive instinct, strive for that with which to debase thought. It seeth the physical appurtenance as that which the Guiding Force hath supplied with which to further growth through the guise of experience. It, through the true valuation, placeth the treasure of the mind, the soul, as that whose intrinsic worth supersedeth all. Therefore of secondary value is that which provideth creature comfort. Man functions in physical being. Therefore the material must provide body with the necessary sustenance; must maintain a state of well-being. It is for this are provided the utilities through which civilization progresseth. He who accepteth the physical manifestation as the gift of the Supreme Creator, diverting his surplus in a humanitarian channel, suffereth not. For the law of proportion apportions to him that which meeteth his every need. Reason, the silent voice of Spirit, it is which guideth soul, indicating the boundary line which separateth the false from the true, the uplifting from the debasing, the idealistic from the adverse.

Oracle Ninety-Three

Knowest thou the reason thy Elder Brother layeth before thee in pristine clarity the frailties to which the flesh is subject? It is that through comprehension of this, the weakness with which thou art afflicted, thou mayest rise above, overcome; that in thy understanding of the remedy thou mayest effect the cure. The remedy lieth within thy grasp. My laws have I given unto thee, that through which soul becometh the purified substance; the transmutation from the impure to the pure spanning the cycle evolution provides. Thou mayest prolong interminably the process employed. Or through comprehension of thy predominating, thy inherent, weakness thou mayest hasten the course. The choice lieth within the individual soul, the bliss of a compensating peace rewarding the renunciation of material desire, of selfish effort. Man learneth that which he hath cast aside representeth but the dross of his yearning. He seeth not the tarnished thread until the golden fabric becometh apparent. Man seeth not the blue ether which lieth beyond the darkened dome of the infinitude. He glimpseth but the darkness, which repelleth. That which lieth beyond unalterable, unchangeable, is. Thus soul through renunciation cometh into that which its disbelief revealeth not. That which thou seest not with thy physical vision existeth. Eternal, it lieth within the spiritual analysis to which thou must of necessity ascend when thy physical existence, brief, impermanent, is complete. No alternative existeth. For the Law through which thy creation became an actuality impelleth thee to make entrance through the Portals of the Infinite, to, in spiritual interpretation, further thy soul's unfoldment. Beloved, thy Elder Brother giveth unto thee these, the unchangeable laws through which thy soul functions.

Absorb thou their content, that in enlightenment thou cast aside the robe in which thy superstition, thy ignorance, enwrappeth thee.

Oracle Ninety-Four

He who entereth the Kingdom of Heaven hath within his own soul erected the altar of the Divine. Thus in worship he giveth homage to the Divine. He hath created the Holy of Holies through which his soul entereth into its rightful heritage. Man speaketh of the Kingdom of Heaven, seeking within the vast infinitude for entrance thereto. Within thee lieth the divine element through which thou becamest a soul. This, the divine element, gave unto thee the nucleus for that which thou art. It provideth the impetus for thought, being the motivating, the impelling, force through which thou givest expression. To deny this, the nucleus of thy being, is to refute the existence of the Supreme God. For within this, His power manifest, camest thou into being. He who through comprehension of the creation of the individual soul giveth unto the Supreme Intelligence the homage, the adoration, through which soul recognizeth the Creator, hath in understanding perpetuated his being. For, as the flint through contact with the steel produceth the light, so Spirit, the divine element which illumineth soul, recognizeth that of which it formeth an integral part. The cosmic force, through which the Supreme Will expresseth, penetrateth each atom; intensifying its initial strength. Thus is impetus given for effort. The cosmic universe it is of which thou art a fractional part. Nature, the Cosmic Mother, demonstrateth this, the supreme power through which gestation taketh place; human, creature, plant—each in like measure responding to the urge she interjects when through procreation the necessity for birth and rebirth becometh apparent. Nature revealeth the intricate and supreme means through which perpetuation taketh place. Unremitting the system employed.

Oracle Ninety-Five

The Golden Precepts have I bestowed upon thee, with which to embellish thy consciousness. As a rosary of priceless value are these, the gems of the Infinite. Accept them, Beloved. Make of them thy thread of prayer through which thy soul weaveth the robe immortal. Unto thee hath come the Master-Healer, that thy wounds through the tincture of His tenderness become receptive to the healing inflow. He hath bathed thy wounds with the essence of His compassion. His love floweth forth to lift thee, to give unto thee that through which mayest thou vision the Light eternal. It is thus He calleth, through the Living Word which speaketh unto thee. Immerse thy soul within this, the Word. For herein lieth the panacea for thy pain. Here alone lieth the Light which faileth not, which maketh of the darkened mind a temple holy and pure. Dedicate thy yearning to that which purifieth, which uplifteth, which draweth thee closer to the shrine of thy being. Immerse thy soul in the Fount of Absolution, which thou mayest find through the subjugation of thy desire. Enter thou the Portals of the Divine through the birth of thy understanding. The Word it is which supporteth thee, for therein lieth all that is. The Word, eternal, supreme, revealeth the working of the Law, which is the Omnipotent Will expressed. Within the Law thou art. And within the Word thou art sustained. The *Book of Life* it is through which the Master speaketh; whereby revelation taketh place, revelation being the illumination through which thy soul cometh into an awareness of the laws beneath which it functions. Thus is bestowed that which formeth the foundation of the Universal Teaching through which the Living Presence becometh manifest; love, understanding, compassion be-

ing the active elements thereof—love which sustaineth;
understanding which precludeth censure, condemnation; and compassion which forgiveth and lifteth. Within the Law lieth the Word. And within the Word lieth
peace. Selah.

Inquiries relating to this work, or to
earlier writings of Aura May Hollen,
among which are—

SONGS OF THE SOUL (*poems*)
THE VINTAGE (*poems*)
LEAVES FROM THE TREE OF LIFE (*prose*)
UNIVERSAL DIMENSION (*prose*)
CONSCIOUSNESS AND ITS PURPOSE (*prose*)

—may be addressed to:

HENRY HOLLEN, M. D.

Brentwood Heights Station   Los Angeles, Calif.